Addiction
and
Recovery

A Practical Guide

By

Rev. Stephen Rodgers, LPC, LMFT
Brian Esparza, M.D., Addictionologist,
MRO, SAP

1

Addiction and Recovery
A practical Guide

Front cover photo: Stephen Rodgers
Back cover photo: Bill Rodgers
Website: Landscapes by Rodgers
Lbwhr.com

Printed through Creative Space
Publisher of Record: Sage Center Publications

ISBN: 978-0692808085

Dedication and Acknowledgments

We want to acknowledge the immense amount of information we have learned from our teachers, colleagues, and from those addicted or impacted by this disease. We hope we have given everyone credit for pieces of information and diagrams we have used.

Dr. Brian Esparza dedicates this book to his wonderful children, Lucia and Mateo

Steve would like to dedicate this to his kids Luke and George, Maggie, the staff at Cedar Hills Hospital—a remarkable group, the parishioners of St. Barnabas Episcopal Church in McMinnville, OR., and all others who have put up with me during the writing of this book

TABLE OF CONTENTS

	Page
Introduction	5
Neurobiology of addiction	7
Medications in addiction	15
Post-Acute Withdrawal Symptoms	19
Another perspective on the brain	22
Things to look for in an addict	46
Process of Change	48
Relapse	55
Where did this all start?	59
Genetics	
Trauma/Abuse/Loss (Grief)	60
Unmet Needs	79
SMARTS—goals	84
The Big 8	87
Myths and truths about addiction	132
Chaos theory as metaphor	142
Self-care, co-dependency, boundaries	174
Co-occurring disorders	189
Triggers and Stressors (stress-cortisol)	191
Values, theory of how life works, 6 circles of identity	204
Neurobiology of the 12 steps	216

Introduction

This book is written primarily for those who live, work, or associate with addicts and those in recovery. While the focus is mostly on drugs and alcohol, the concepts are true of any addiction that impacts your/their lives. Whenever we use the words you/your/their, understand that any of those can potentially fit into any sentence. The disease of substance dependency impacts all those around addicts/recovering addicts. This book can also work for addicts who want to understand what is going on and how to help themselves.

There is nothing radically new in this book. What we have tried to do is gather all the important information and put it into a language people can understand and use. Theory in and of itself has never helped anyone. It is how those theories, ideas, and information are used that helps.

While we encourage people to start at the beginning, you can find specific issues of recovery and addiction in the table of contents.

We will look at what is going on inside the addict's brain—literally. We will look at some of the large issues for them and how you can help them. We will offer some ideas about how to take care of yourself. The more we understand the addicted brain, the more effectively we can assist in recovery.

You will find that we are at times very blunt. Addiction wants to play games and as long as the games are played, the addict and everyone around them lose.

Life is full of difficult choices. Our desire is that your life is filled with self-respect and that you find the tools necessary to help those in recovery on their journey. Virtually every person on Planet Earth is impacted by someone with addiction. The challenge is how to respond to them.

Our response will obviously be different depending on who the person is and how we are "related" to them. We will hopefully deal differently with a spouse than someone we barely know or a boss. Being mindful of how we interact with the addicted matters because we can be and often are part of the problem. This does not let them off the hook, but we do need to look at ourselves while looking at them. Addiction comes from somewhere. We still have few clues as to why some people fall into addiction and others with similar backgrounds, issues, and genetics don't.

Addiction is one of the most costly and brutal diseases on Planet Earth. People have been trying to find answers and solutions for well over a century. Untold billions of dollars and some of the best minds on Earth have gone into finding answers and few, if any, have been found. We understand to a large degree what it is in the brain, but how it happened at its outset and how to stop it are still a mystery. Those who believe there is a cure are lying to you. Permanent remission is possible; a cure is not—to date.

As is true with addicts, recovery comes with action. If you do nothing, nothing will change. We offer many ways of changing your thinking and acting to help yourself and the addict in recovery. If they do not follow through on these, they (and probably you) will repeat the cycle they have probably gone through before.

The American Society of Addiction Medicine defines addiction as "...a primary, chronic disease of brain reward, motivation, memory and related circuitry." Addiction is considered a chronic disease characterized by craving and loss of control. This book seeks to help others understand this disease and how to be of assistance to others in keeping the disease in remission.

You will see that we look at addiction from a wide variety of angles. Shame, unmet needs, and chaos theory are but a few. We hope you will gain insight into your situation and those of the people around you.

Substance Addiction versus Other Addictions

This book is focused on chemical dependency, but the same ideas are relevant to all addictions. Here are some criteria used to assess a wide variety of addictions. Internet addiction and others may not have the same physical signs of chemical dependency, but the other consequences more often than not are associated, and recovery strategies also fall in line with substance addictions.

These came from the main article posted at:
http://www.ncbi.nlm.nih.gov/pmc/articles/PMC3354400/

-Salience: Domination of a person's life by the activity
-Euphoria: A 'buzz' or a 'high' is derived from the activity
-Tolerance: The activity has to be undertaken to a progressively greater extent to achieve the same 'buzz'
-Withdrawal Symptoms: Cessation of the activity leads to the occurrence of unpleasant emotions or physical effects
-Conflict: The activity leads to conflict with others or self-conflict
-Relapse and Reinstatement: Resumption of the activity with the same vigor subsequent to attempts to abstain, negative life consequences, and negligence of job, educational or career opportunities.

Remember that addicts are brilliant at explaining away each of these.

Two neurobiological ways of looking at addiction: The technical and the practical

The Technical Side

Your brain has over 100 billion neuron cells that contain over 2 trillion--that's 2,000,000,000,000--connections. In the end, how our brains are wired determines what we do, think, and say. One way of looking at addiction or chemical dependency is to see that the brain has been hijacked, rewired (literally) to revolve around the disease. This chapter will show how that process takes place and how it impacts how the brain works.

This first section is technical. We will keep it as simple as possible to make the point and if you want to delve further into this, there are a wide variety of sources that discuss the neurobiology of addiction (a few are listed at the end). The next chapter will look into why this process gets started.

Unless you are born addicted, your brain is wired in such a way that normal daily activities make you feel good. People do not enjoy being unhappy, angry, depressed, or fearful. When we do things like exercise, eat well, have purpose and meaning in our lives, and do things that are fun by ourselves and/or with others, our brains make a variety of neurotransmitters that send a signal to our emotional and thinking centers that says "feel good!!" Unconsciously, our brains are rewarding us for doing those activities. We want to feel good so we do them again, and we are psychologically rewarded for doing good and healthy things. Here is a list of the neurotransmitters and what they are associated with:

Dopamine: Euphoria, pleasure, mood, motor function
Serotonin: Mood, impulsivity, anxiety, sleep, cognition (thinking)
Endorphins, Enkephalins: lessening of the feeling of pain
GABA: Anxiety, panic, relaxation

The neurons in your brain have endpoints and there is a gap between the endpoint of one neuron and the starting of another. This is called the synapse. Neurotransmitters transmit information between the synapses, sending the message extremely rapidly across these circuits. On the neurons are receptors. Each type of receptor has a unique shape which only certain shaped molecules can attach to. When you are having a great time, you create messages that manufacture these neurotransmitters. They in turn attach to the neuron receptor sites and send the message to feel pleasure by triggering the production of dopamine. We are rewarded by feeling pleasure that spurs us on to repeat that cycle. The beginning of this process starts with the ventral tegmental area or VTA. The VTA sends a message to the nucleus accumbens, which then distributes signals to a variety of other areas of the brain that get people to use. Here is one diagram that very simply shows the process for alcohol.

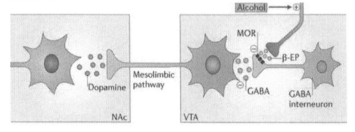

Nature Reviews | Neuroscience

http://neurowiki2012.wikispaces.com/Treatment?showComments=1

Another diagram shows a more broad picture of addiction and how complicated this gets.

http://img.medscape.com/article/838/083/838083-fig1.jpg

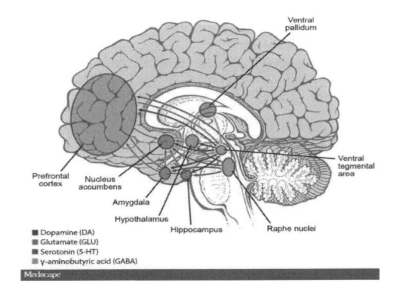

It turns out that other "drugs" attach to these receptors. The shape of alcohol, opioids, benzos, cannabis and others have unique shapes that attach to these sites, release dopamine (because that is the message they send) and make us feel good, relaxed, pain free, less anxious, etc. This is how addiction gets started. We become rewarded by using. Ongoing use triggers the reward mechanism and makes us feel "better" in the moment. We do not understand fully why some people move from this state into one of dependence and why some don't. Some may have deficient neurotransmitters to begin with, or an inability to create them. If a person is sober for a year and still does not feel pleasure, they may want to have a doctor look into this aspect of their brain chemistry.

One of the problems is that your brain does not want that all the time; it does not want to be in a dopamine-producing state of being full blast all the time. When people use, that is what they are doing, making their brain go into overdrive to secrete these neurotransmitters to help them feel good. Every drug does something different between synapses. Meth, for example, will push large amounts of dopamine into the synapse and then go back and block the receptors on the dopamine producing neuron. Dopamine usually sends its message and then goes back. Meth floods the synapse. The brain can't handle it all so it makes more receptors--which have to be fed. When we consistently over-stimulate the receptors they expect to be fed constantly. When there is no substance giving them what they want, they get mad. The increase of receptors and the flooding of current receptors with the expectation that more dopamine will be created create a larger need for the substance--tolerance.

When a baby cries at first it might drive us crazy, but we adapt to the sounds. Someone else comes into the house and you can see how jarring the crying is to them. Our receptors become a bit complacent over time; the amount of a substance used doesn't carry the same weight it used to. Our brains get used to feeling "normal" on a certain amount of a substance, but as the receptors increase and flood we need more to feel normal. You will often hear addicts state that they need to use just to feel normal. They aren't lying; the problem is that what normal is has changed. When an addict "gets well" (sober), the receptors start screaming to be fed--cravings and withdrawal. Because the brain is attached to everything, addiction in craving and withdrawal mode triggers physical reactions to try to get the person to use again to satiate the receptors and the brain. Sweats, cramps, shakes, and seizures are but a few of the conditions we equate with withdrawal. Untreated, these symptoms can be quite serious and, with alcohol and benzodiazepines, can lead to death. The safest way to detox or withdraw from any substance is under medical care. The majority of those who attempt to detox themselves fail.

If you look above at what the neurotransmitters transmit, withdrawal is the opposite. Lack of dopamine leads to dysphoria, loss of purpose, feeling ill, and becoming anxious and irritable. The addiction is seeking to reward the user by making them feel better when they use, a positive reward from the perspective of the addiction. Withdrawal creates a negative reward by the symptoms of withdrawal and the increase of what was just mentioned. Given a choice in the moment, we should not be surprised the dependent person seeks the positive reward. **The goal of recovery is to switch those and create a positive reward system for sobriety and a negative one for using.**

Every person is different as to their tolerance level and the impact of withdrawal. There are correlations with age, number of relapses, amounts used and in the body, how physically fit a person is, and a host of psychiatric issues that impact addiction.

There is no black and white line as to when a person crosses from use to abuse to dependency; they are gray areas. Dependency is what it says: when a person becomes dependent on something. We look for signs of withdrawal, increased tolerance, and how their use has impacted their physical, social, work, spiritual, cognitive, and emotional lives. In general it is better to be safe than sorry. Better to err on the side of being dependent or heading into that state than to feel that all is well. You do not have to use four times a day or even daily to be addicted. Binge users can be addicts; they are still dependent on the binge.

There is also no set timeline for detoxing substances. It depends on the substance, how much is being used, and for how long. The goal in a medically monitored detox is to rid the body of the chemical causing the withdrawal while not having the person be in agony. There are a variety of medications physicians use to accomplish this. Some reduce the possibilities of seizures; others block the receptor sites so the artificial message to feel good is no longer present. Still others will help level out anxiety or lift depression. In the end, the body must metabolize and rid itself of the chemicals. It's important to remember that when the chemicals are gone, the receptors are still there and are very hungry. Normally, in a hospital, detoxing takes 7-10 days. This is just to rid the body of the addicted chemical. The brain is far from rewired—that takes at least 3-6 months if the person does everything that needs to be done.

One of the reasons people relapse is because their minds have been focused on and revolve around the addiction, getting the next "fix." Our brains do not rewire overnight. This need and the cravings can be intense for months. Receptors need to establish a semblance of "normalcy," where creative and healthy activities replace destructive unhealthy ones.

It is important to remember that the receptors that have been activated in addiction do not die in recovery;

13

they essentially go dormant. Our dendrites, part of the neurons, develop dendritic spines or bumps, memories that communicate across the neural network. They increase in size and permanency over time. Addicts have these bumps that are triggered by things in their lives. They become permanent over time, but the degree to which they are impacted by stimuli and communicate with each other diminishes with the length of time of recovery. When someone relapses after a long period of time, the receptors and the spines are all activated and reconnected at an astonishing rate. This is why most addicts in relapse pick up where they left off in a very short time, no matter how long it's been. Here is a picture of the bumps. A short video about them is available at this website.
https://www.youtube.com/watch?v=xMiFNmemNyM

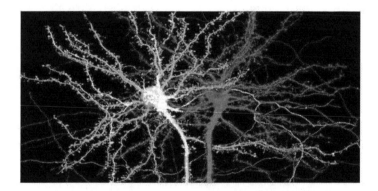

Here is a book that speaks to what we have just said in much greater detail.

-- "Hijacking the Brain" by Louis Teresi, MD., and Harry Haroutunian, MD.

Medications

Doctors can give prescriptions that can aid people in withdrawal and in reducing cravings until the brain has rewired itself for recovery. Here is a brief list of medications used and what they do:

Suboxone: A partial antagonist of the opiate receptor that helps stabilize symptoms of detoxification. If an individual is opiate dependent, the use of suboxone will not create a sense of euphoria, due to the blockage of the mu component of the opiate receptor. There are two approaches to the use of suboxone, a harm reduction model where a patient will remain on a low dose for an extended period of time and a gradual dose reduction. The use of suboxone can be a valuable tool in that it allows patients to engage in therapy/recovery treatment because they are not in active detoxification, nor intoxicated.

The expectation of therapy is a requirement of suboxone treatment. Suboxone does not create an emotional barrier, therefore there is often a tsunami of emotions in early recovery. Individuals in recovery may not be prepared for the emotional, financial and at times legal consequences of their drug use. This is therefore a high relapse time in recovery that must be addressed in therapy.

Methadone: A full agonist of the opiate receptor is often used for individuals with significant opiate dependence and chronic pain issues. Methadone may be a very lethal medication in overdose and is therefore highly controlled and regulated. The majority of patients that are on methadone are in an opiate replacement or harm reduction treatment model. Dosages are often provided on a daily basis and urine drug screens are closely monitored.

Naltrexone: Naltrexone works at the level of the nucleus accumbens by decreasing the release of dopamine and therefore effectively reducing the cravings to use opiates. In addition, it serves as an antagonist, or blocker of the opiate receptor. Naltrexone does have a long-acting preparation called vivitrol which will effectively block the opiate receptor for a 30-day period. The importance of naltrexone is that it does not have any addictive properties and therefore will not cause withdrawal with the discontinuation of use. This feature is in direct contrast to both methadone and suboxone, which have potentially addictive properties that may lead to relapse if abruptly discontinued.

    The benefits of naltrexone extend beyond opiates. Once again, since this medication works at the level of the nucleus accumbens, or the reward pathway, its application has been extended to alcohol dependency, methamphetamine dependency, and pathological gambling.

Antabuse: Used in the treatment of alcohol dependence by creating an adverse reaction in the patient if they drink alcohol. Antabuse (disulfiram) inhibits the degradation of acetaldehyde in the liver, which ultimately builds up and creates nausea, vomiting, sweating, flushing of the face, anxiety and weakness. This adverse reaction often will serve to prevent alcoholics from relapsing. It is important, however, to understand that this medication is often reserved for highly motivated patients, as it must be taken on a daily basis. Compliance with Antabuse is increased if the patient is actively monitored taking their medication. In addition, Antabuse, in contrast to naltrexone, does not reduce cravings to drink but simply punishes the patient for relapsing.

Campral: Used in the treatment of alcohol dependence, Campral is felt to work on stabilizing the balance between GABA and glutamate. Early recovery from alcohol is often accompanied by a wave of rebound anxiety. The use of Campral in patients with a comorbid anxiety disorder has demonstrated therapeutic value.

Patients should always consult with a doctor when coming off any medication. Coming off a medication too quickly often leads to a relapse and can be potentially life threatening.

It should be noted that with all these medications, some type of ongoing therapy is suggested. With Suboxone, some type of therapy is required. The idea is that medications give the brain the ability to rewire, which can't happen while actively using. The underlying issues need to be dealt with for long term remission. People do have withdrawal symptoms from these medications, depending on how much they are taking and how quickly they come off them. Patients should always consult with a doctor when coming off any medication. Coming off a medication too quickly often leads to a relapse and can be potentially life threatening.

In short, people use to increase euphoria, freedom from pain (physical and/or emotional), and to relieve stress. As they move to dependency they use to avoid withdrawal and dysphoria. They lose the desire and motivation to do what it takes to feed the receptors in more normative ways--it's easier to just use. Eventually the brain stops making dopamine and the addict must use almost constantly to maintain any internal sense of normalcy. In order to do this they are willing to do whatever it takes, including lying, cheating, stealing, manipulating, and leaving a destructive path in their wake. Internally and temporarily they are rewarded--addiction seeks to use the reward system wired in the brain to motivate people to use more. Rewards work. I've never met a gifted musician who hated every minute of practice it took to become phenomenal at what they do. Internally they are rewarded for their long and often painful practice. They are also rewarded by seeing the joy better musicians than they get for their hard work. Addicts often see the "fun" and lack of stress other users have and their brains use that as a reward.

Post-acute withdrawal symptoms

People can have PAWS—Post-acute withdrawal symptoms. This means that weeks or months after a person has detoxed, their brains can trick them into having the symptoms of withdrawal. What do most people do when they have withdrawal symptoms? They use. Most of the time these symptoms are not as intense, nor do they last as long. They are not actually in withdrawal.

Making the assumption that someone has used is not helpful; being aware of PAWS is. Support the person through this time. It's better that they not be alone because temptation will be very high. Encourage the person to share with you when they are having a PAWS event.

Here is a bit more on PAWS:

There are two stages of withdrawal. The first stage is the acute stage, which usually lasts at most a few days to a couple of weeks. During this stage, the person in recovery experiences physical withdrawal symptoms. But every drug is different, and every person is different.

The second stage of withdrawal is called the Post-Acute Withdrawal Syndrome (PAWS). During this stage they will have fewer physical symptoms (although they do occur), but more emotional and psychological withdrawal symptoms.

Post-acute withdrawal occurs because your brain chemistry is gradually returning to normal. As your brain improves the levels of your brain chemicals fluctuate as they approach the new equilibrium, causing post-acute withdrawal symptoms.

Most people experience some post-acute withdrawal symptoms. There are similarities in both detox and post-acute withdrawal. The intensity and parts of the body or life that are impacted differ with each person.

The Symptoms of Post-Acute Withdrawal
The most common post-acute withdrawal symptoms are:
- Mood swings
- Anxiety
- Irritability
- Tiredness
- Variable energy
- Low enthusiasm
- Variable concentration
- Disturbed sleep

Post-acute withdrawal feels like a rollercoaster of symptoms. In the beginning, the symptoms may change minute to minute and hour to hour. Later, as they recover further, symptoms will disappear for a few weeks or months, only to potentially return again. This is not an excuse for using or for poor behavior; it's meant to give an understanding of what is going on in their brains.

Each post-acute withdrawal episode usually lasts from hours to a few days. Once a person has been in recovery for a while, you will find that each post-acute withdrawal episode usually lasts for a less time. There is no obvious trigger for most episodes. They will wake up one day feeling irritable and have low energy. If they hang on, it will lift just as quickly as it started. After a while they'll develop confidence that they can get through post-acute withdrawal, because they'll know that each episode is time limited. It is important to know ahead of time what they will do when one of these takes place because the addict often resorts to using to stop withdrawal symptoms—real or perceived.

Post-acute withdrawal can last for up to two years. This is one of the most important things you need to remember. If they're up for the challenge they can get through this. But if you or they think that post-acute withdrawal will only last for a few months, then you'll get caught off guard, and when they're disappointed they're more likely to relapse. (Reference: AddictionsAndRecovery.org)

How to Survive Post-Acute Withdrawal

Be patient. Don't sit around waiting for PAWS to happen, just be aware. For many it never happens. Accusing someone of using when it is PAWS only leads them to say to themselves, "Why bother trying? They are always going to think I'm using." If you truly feel they have relapsed and they are denying it you might try saying the following: "Sue, I'm feeling uncomfortable right now. I know it could be PAWS but I think you may have relapsed. Would you be willing to do a drug screen to prove me wrong?" You are not blaming them, you are accepting responsibility and asking for their help to prove you wrong. If you are wrong, after the test admit to it. If they refuse, the chances are high they have relapsed. You can buy inexpensive test kits at a drug store.

We suggest having this conversation early on in recovery. Share with them your concerns about relapse, PAWS, and the impact of their using again on your life (especially if you are living with them). Part of this is about the person helping. We can't be watching over them all the time, expecting them to relapse. We can't ask them every day to give a sample when over and over they are clean. It's your brain that needs changing too.

By now it is probably obvious what helps keep PAWS at bay and helps the person get through them quickly--The Big 8 will be discussed in another chapter.

We need to end the story on a more positive note. *Recovery can lead to sustained remission from the drug of choice, a change in the reward pathway in the brain to more creative and healthy solutions, return to full brain function (unless permanent damage has been done), and a sense of hope, purpose, and contentment. It's a choice. Addiction is a disease of choice.*

For a more detailed look at this try:
http://www.nap.edu/read/5802/chapter/5
 https://www.youtube.com/watch?v=BpHiFqXCYKc--Gabor Mate

ANOTHER NEUROBIOLOGICAL WAY OF SEEING ADDICTION

Above we talked about the reward system in the brain and some of the more technical parts of that process. Now we would like to look at five significant parts of the brain that are negatively impacted by addiction. We will be talking in general statements here because every person responds and reacts differently to being addicted and/or being impacted by it. These areas are impacted by all forms of addiction, chemical or other.

Cognition-Thinking—Our frontal cortex is the main part of the brain that helps us think. If you can't think you are a vegetable and do nothing. Some of us can't turn our thinking off; it seems to go 24 hours a day. Some people's thoughts are highly confused or out of touch with reality, as we see with Dementia, Alzheimer's, psychosis, delusions, or paranoia. The majority of humans can focus, think clearly (not necessarily accurately), track a conversation, and make sense, most of the time. We all have our moments. Addiction skews each of those thinking areas. We have all been around a drunken person who can't focus, whose ideas make no sense, who loses track of what is being talked about, and whose voice and thinking are slurred. To differing degrees this is true of all chemically addicted behaviors. The brain struggles to maintain composure but the amount of any given drug in their brain does not allow that to happen. They believe they are fine; the observer knows better.

The addict tries to rationalize everything. There is always a reason for the next fix. "I'm lonely, I'm in pain, it's Arbor Day, because I can" are all reasons people use. None of them is a good reason. Their thinking has become corrupted. In Cognitive Behavior Therapy (CBT) they call this Cognitive Distortions or Thinking Errors. We all have them; addicts just tend to have more and have them at a deeper level. These distortions distort reality so what our brain wants to think and see makes sense.

Here are ten examples of distorted thinking.

1. **All-or-nothing thinking** – Everything is black and white; there is little to no gray. When someone relapses on one beer they will say to themselves, "I failed, screw it," and go all the way, sometimes for months. They could have said, "I had one, I know what will happen if I continue, let me call my sponsor or friend and nip this in the bud." They don't. They might make you feel guilty by saying, "A true friend would understand and stand with me, but you won't, so I guess you aren't a true friend." We know this is not true; the addicted brain does not.

2. **Overgeneralization** – When you hear words like "always" and "never," this is overgeneralization. They take an event and make it sound like that is the totality of life. "I had a bad day at work, I'm just not a good teacher, why bother?" Addicts may say, "I will always be an addict." This is true, but they could say, "I am an addict in remission and I plan on staying that way." Statements like "I will never use again," or "I will always call you when I get stressed" are dangerous. How do they know?

3. **Mental Filter** – A lot of us have this one. Someone gives you many compliments about your life or work and then throws in one "criticism" at the end. What do you remember? Users use the negatives in life (sometimes not even a reality) to justify their using. "She always criticizes me." All of these filters can start at a very young age. When

we are humiliated as a child, that is what our brain hears. It sabotages life in order to prove those statements true. If parents tell you as a child you are stupid, there is a tendency to do poorly in school to show them they are right—and they have evidence to keep saying it. Addiction filters out the positives of life and the negatives of addiction.

4. Discounting the positive - You reject positive experiences by insisting that they "don't count." This leads to shame because we begin to think we are not worthy. Addiction doesn't want people having a valid positive self-image. It loves a false positive self-image. It wants them to see that in spite of their using they are amazing; it's the using that helps. Enablers tend to supply this. All of us need to learn to accept compliments and raise the positives in our lives.

5. Jumping to conclusions - You interpret things negatively when there are no facts to support your conclusion.

Mind Reading: We know what people are thinking, especially the negatives and critical thoughts. We base our response to them on what we "know" to be true—even when it isn't. We don't take the time or energy to check out our assumptions.

Fortune-telling: This is very common with addicts. "I've relapsed before, I will probably relapse again." "I've never been able to handle stress, I won't now." "All my friends are going to judge me; they won't be there to help." All of these are statements that set the person up for failure.

6. Magnification – Mountains out of molehills or molehills out of mountains. Addicts do this in order to justify using. They minimize the negative and magnify the positive.

7. Emotional Reasoning – We have thinking and emotional brains. The brain wants to find a balance. When emotions take over, they rule the roost. We feel that reality is what our emotions say. "I'm depressed, therefore all is bad and will only get worse." "I did something wrong, therefore I'm a horrible person." "I'm angry, so the person that made me angry must be bad and wrong." Balance allows the rational brain to check the emotions against the evidence.

8. "Should" statements – Should have, could have, ought to, have to are all statements that get us in trouble, especially addicts. They lead to guilt, frustration, and anger. Words are important; they internally and externally form our actions.

There is a subtle difference between saying, "I should exercise," and "I know my brain would be helped if I exercise." "You should stop drinking," is different than "It would be helpful to me and our relationship if your drinking would stop; is there anything I can do to help with that?" One is judgmental, one is helpful.

Dr. Albert Ellis, one of the founders of CBT, has called this "must-erbation."

9. Labeling – We all label things to some degree. We stereotype certain people. We put ourselves in a box with a label. "I'm a loser," "I'm an addict," "I'm brilliant" are all labeling statements. These labels block the totality of reality. There are exceptions to virtually every stereotype, usually more than we care to admit. It's ok to say "I am an addict," as long as that is not all you are. When working with the addicted that is a lens we view them through. Just make sure it isn't the only lens, for they are far more than just an addict and it is that "other" that we need to help raise up and develop.

10. Personalization and Blame – The blame game is seen a lot in addiction. It's part of the denial process. "If you wouldn't yell at me I wouldn't drink." "My job is so stressful I need to relax." They may internalize the blame: "I'm an addict, I do nothing but destroy, and it won't change." As long as people are unwilling to accept reality and their part in it, nothing will change. In recovery, the blame game has to stop. Yes, there are reasons people use, but there are no excuses because there is always an alternative way to deal with the realities they face--others have found a way; so can they.

Ten Ways to Untwist Your Thinking

1. **Identify The Distortion:** Which distortions do you or they have? Admitting to them is the first step. We can't fix what we don't see or admit to.

2. **Examine the Evidence:** Use both the rational and emotional brain to check the evidence. If you were in court would there be enough evidence to validate what you are thinking? Are you willing to share that evidence with someone else (someone who will tell you that you are full of it) to have them act as a check and balance to your thinking? Is an alcoholic willing to go to someone in long term recovery or someone who understands addiction and say, "I'm feeling good; I know I can handle just one beer?" They don't ask because they know the answer.

3. **The Double-Standard Method:** Help them learn that self-talk matters. Do they talk to themselves in the same way they speak to others? If you hear them being overly harsh on themselves, ask them if they would say that to someone else.

4. **The Experimental Technique:** Everything in this book is "experimental." What have they tried and how many times? We hear often with people in relapse, "I went to a meeting, it didn't work and I

didn't like it." They have generalized one meeting to all meetings and have not given that experiment a chance. How many musicians would we have on the planet if everyone quit the first time they played the instrument and weren't perfect? None. Whatever we do, we need to do often to build the habit. That is what addiction did. They gave addiction a shot; now it's time to give recovery a shot.

5. Thinking in Shades of Gray: At times things are black and white. The earth is either flat or not. But in life, gray is more common. When you hear the person in recovery speaking in black and white language, challenge it; find the gray. While there is a harm reduction model of addiction which allows for some use, zero use is the best and most effective model for recovery. Shades of gray as to using can lead to addiction and relapse.

6. The Survey Method: Other people are one of the critical keys to recovery. If you/they are unwilling to check out your ideas with others, there is probably a cognitive error involved. This does not mean you have to agree with what others say, but at least you are willing to listen.

7. Define Terms: Words matter. What do people mean with what they say? Even the word addict has different meanings to different people. Have conversations around words and ideas to make sure you understand and are understood.

8. The Semantic Method: Again, words matter. The words we choose have a greater impact on others than we like to admit. Listen to them. How do they talk about addiction and recovery? How do they verbalize their feelings about themselves?

9. Re-attribution: Instead of just saying, "I'm an addict," what led to this moment? What things need to be worked on? What relationships avoided? What behaviors need to change? What of the Big 8 needs effort? Put the focus and energy on getting better.

10. Cost-Benefit Analysis: This is the pros and cons method. We know that addicts use for a reason: there is a benefit, a reward, for doing it. They don't take time to assess the cons and costs. Feelings, thoughts, and actions have benefits and costs. At times it's helpful to look at those.

Some people see alcoholics as bums and street people. That is their reality. We all know it isn't true; that is a stereotype. For some reason that person wants/needs to see it that way; it helps them organize their world view.

At some point in the progression of addiction the addict's brain will start to say things like, "I can never overcome my addiction so why bother?" "I've always been an addict; I will always be an addict." "I have a lot of reasons I use and they aren't going to change, so why stop?" "I've tried everything, I've relapsed too many times, and there is no hope." "I have no one in my life to help me and I can't do it alone." "I don't remember a time I didn't use; this is what I know." To the person saying these, they are true. Hopefully the person reading this can look at each statement and see the flaw within each. When a person finds stability, remission, and recovery, these statements disappear and the addict can look back and laugh at what their brains convinced them of.

The brain has been hijacked, on all levels. The brain convinces the addict they aren't really lying, cheating, stealing, or manipulating; they are simply avoiding an unnecessary confrontation with people that don't understand. "I just need to relax, break through my inhibitions, laugh a bit more, have some fun, forget about the stressors in my life for a while, not feel the pain in my body, escape the depression or anxiety, or take a break from the world." These are the reasons the brain tells an addict they need the fix. We do not deny that all of those may be valid; we just believe they can have all those without using. There are creative answers to the issues in one's life other than to become addicted.

In recovery the addict needs to challenge their thinking mind. They need to catch themselves thinking and making statements that are not true. Lack of honesty to self and others is a hallmark of all addiction. In recovery they must face the truth and proclaim it. Addicts will continue to distort reality in recovery, and they need to be open with someone who can challenge their thoughts. At six months some alcoholics will say, "I've been clean for six months; I can handle a beer." Are they willing to look someone in the eye who understands addiction or who has been in recovery for years and tell them that? Rarely, because they know those people will laugh. They don't share some of their thoughts because they already know the answer they will get back, and that isn't what the brain wants to hear.

Those helping people in recovery need to be curious. We need to ask questions that will enable the person to be open about what they are thinking and feeling in their lives. The human brain is wired to share; it wants connection because it knows the traps we fall into if we don't have the checks and balances system of other people. Usually before a relapse you will see the addicted thinking brain kick in. They will make statements that are already starting to justify using again in their minds--the better if they can get you to buy in. A good response to those types of statements might be, "Bill, that statement makes me think you are considering using again. We both know that is a choice you can make. I am here to help you with recovery, not addiction. I admit I might be misreading what you are saying, but that is what it sounds like to me." They may get defensive, but their brain has received the challenge and is well aware someone out there is onto them. That in and of itself helps the recovery brain know it has support.

We all know the difference between positive thinking and negative thinking. Help the addict focus on positive things. What can they read, who can they have conversations with, and what can they do to support recovery and take power away from addiction? While AA does tell sordid tales of addiction, the focus is on recovery and how to find it. What brings true purpose and meaning to the addict? Most addicts have lost a deep sense of purpose and meaning in their lives because addiction has become the purpose. We can help people in recovery discover or rediscover a sense of purpose in their lives. Purpose brings meaning and hope, critical ingredients for long term recovery and for a healthy life.

Emotions-Feelings—The amygdala is the primary seat of our emotions, although several other areas are involved. When all is working well, our emotions act as a check and balance to our thinking. In DBT (Dialectical Behavior Therapy), when our emotional and rational sides work in tandem, we achieve wisdom, or wise mind. When we ignore our emotions, we are ignoring our brains--not a wise thing to do. When our emotions are out of control, we lose the sense of thinking, and the distortions become significant.

When asked what happens to their emotions when they are using, most addicts will tell you they either go flat or are exaggerated. Chemicals and behaviors affect our emotions, we all know that. When we become dependent on chemicals or some behaviors, the pathways in our brains change.

Human beings grow and develop throughout their lives: mentally, physically, and emotionally. Maturity in part has to do with how we emotionally respond to situations. Addiction freezes our emotional state during the progression of the disease. People who become addicted in adolescence stay emotionally adolescent. As with other neural aspects impacted by addiction, a person's emotional maturity or intelligence can be repaired as well.

People with addiction issues often have emotional issues that add to reasons they become addicted. People will use because they are depressed, fearful, anxious, or angry. It temporarily soothes them and helps them avoid reality. You may know someone who avoids their emotions—not a healthy way to treat your brain in the long run. Our brains are created to regulate emotions; when they become unregulated for an extended period of time, something is wrong. It may be something other than addiction, but that is something people should be aware of and look into. When people make emotional mountains out of molehills, the same is true.

Our amygdala and emotional systems in the brain are working all the time; there is an emotional response to virtually everything that goes on around us, even if slight. There are layers of emotions that are built up with knowledge, memories, habits, and addiction.

It's important to understand the difference between emotion, feeling and mood. We often equate them, but they are different. For our purposes here is an easy way to think about them:

Emotions—A chemical response to a trigger. Our brains are triggered by some event that affects one or more of our senses--a television commercial about beer, for example. Within a quarter of a second your brain identifies the trigger and tells the rest of the body it's time to respond. Within another quarter of a second the body releases chemicals to deal with the fear, joy, anger, or other core emotions. A true emotional response does not last long.

Feelings—Once our bodies have emotionally responded, the brain starts to work with all the information around that trigger to elicit a feeling. The brain uses memory, reason, current environmental circumstances, and a general sense of the current emotional state. Emotions are raw and chemically oriented; feelings are more integrated with our thoughts. Feelings can last for a long period of time.

Mood—Our moods are influenced by our current state of emotions, the environment around us, physical state of being, and what we eat. Moods can last a long time. A person who is "moody" gets stuck. If you look at their lives, there may be no reason for them to be feeling that way; they have created a worldview at that time that seems real to them. They may have reasons for feeling the way they do but aren't doing anything to change the situation; they are stuck as well.

Addiction tends to elicit a sense of being stuck. They are not growing emotionally because the pathway in their brain is very narrowly focused. Addiction uses emotions to its advantage. When you are using, you feel more relaxed and carefree; negative emotions slow down or disappear. You are rewarded for using on an emotional-feeling level. When you stop, all the negative emotions and feelings come back; there is no reward. Why would someone not use if it makes those emotions and feelings disappear?

We want the addict to understand this process and trap that has been created and to know there is a way out. Remember that addiction is about instant gratification. Recovery is about extended, long-term gratification. They need to see the big picture, to see how their using negatively impacts life around them and keeps them in the never-ending cycle the reward system creates in their brain. So while the person in recovery is giving their brain a chance to think more clearly and to face reality, recovery also gives them a chance to face their emotions and feelings and the triggers that bring them forth. Recovery gives the brain a chance to grow and adapt to reality in a creative and healthy way.

As those working with the addicted, we can help them by:

1. Acknowledging our own emotions and feelings. "When you use, I feel _____ (angry, sad, frustrated, and depressed)." We need to own our own emotions. This is not about blame.
2. Help them talk about what they are feeling and where that is coming from. Help them to own their own emotions.
3. Send them to a DBT class; what they learn there will help.
4. In recovery help them to see that if there are underlying emotional issues, they aren't going to just disappear by themselves, and they will need to get help to work through them.
5. Do things to help build positive emotions--have fun, do things that bring forth meaning in their lives. This is not about shame and guilt, but about finding the value in that person when they aren't using and helping them to see how that disappears when addiction is in action.

Obviously none of this work can take place while a person is using; it's a mostly wasted effort. Get them clear and stable and encourage them to take on the hard work to put the addiction into permanent remission.

Senses—There are five senses: sight, hearing, smell, taste and touch. All of them are impaired by addiction. Ultimately, it is our senses that move a person into dependency. The brain acquires information to make decisions from our senses. You can't have a memory without senses—at least initially. Our senses other than smell (which is wired directly to the frontal cortex— thinking part) are wired to the thalamus. It directs the sensory input to the other parts of the brain, depending on what it determines is needed. The thalamus is impacted by neural pathways that have already been created. Imagine if we take away all five senses--what would happen to you? We would all die very quickly because we wouldn't feel hungry, and we wouldn't know if we were communicating with anyone about anything.

Think about what triggers the person to use. If you don't know, ask them; they will know. Triggers are memories that are brought to consciousness by a sense experience. An addiction trigger activates the reward system instantly and the person has little choice on their own but to use. An example is a woman at the hospital who was addicted to wine. She got to a point in her addiction where she could not walk down the dairy aisle (with the wine right across from it) without putting wine in the cart. Her mind would create a list and her style of shopping would make her go down the aisle a few times every time she visited the store. The sight of the wine triggered the brain to reach for the wine. She wasn't sure how to stop. We told her when she went down the aisle to go with someone who wouldn't let her put wine in the basket—create memories based on the senses that changed how the trigger was perceived in the brain. She reported that after a couple of months and going up and down the aisle a couple of hundred times, she no longer had any interest in reaching for the wine.

To help an addict's senses we can:

1. Assist them in recovery to discover triggers and what the sense is that is used. What can be done to change the impact of the sense on the trigger? How can you support them in that effort?

2. Create new sense-oriented experiences. Think every day of what you can taste that will bring joy to your palate, what you can see and explore with your eyes that will lift your spirits, what you can smell that will soothe your mind, what you can touch that will please the skin, and what you can hear that will stimulate your mind in healthy ways. If the addict can create meaningful sense experiences that are healthy and relaxing, after a time their brains will gravitate to the new experience more than to the old habits.

3. All of us should pay more attention to our senses, using them and becoming more fully consciously aware of them in our lives. Use them in your conversations; become aware of and talk about tone, tastes, smells, sights, and feelings of touch. We have our senses for a reason; they help ground us in the world about us. We know that when we lose a sense others are able to adapt to a certain degree. The key is using what we have to create a different sense of the world than what addiction has given that person.

Memories--From early in life we gather information and create memories. Those memories come from thoughts, emotions, and senses, three of the key parts of our brains that we know are impacted by addiction. If our thinking, emotions, and senses are changed in the process of addiction, then we shouldn't be surprised that our memories are as well.

We have already discussed how all people have a distorted view of reality. This is only enhanced by the disease of addiction. Many of us stand in awe of how someone in the throes of addiction can retell an event they were at and have such a different view than ours. They forget most if not all negative details. They minimize consequences. "I wasn't driving that bad; the officer was having a bad night." "Bill and Sue are having some issues in their marriage, not sure why they had to pick on me." "Maybe I didn't need to hit Tom, but he pissed me off." "Yes, I'd been drinking, but not that much, not enough to make John leave me."

It's one of the reasons having an intervention works. There are people in the room who will challenge the memories of the addicted—to their face. Do not be afraid to challenge a memory. There is a chance that something in your life may have distorted a memory as well. So be it. This is why we stick to facts.

The intensity, depth, and impact of a memory are created either by repetition or initial intensity. One way of looking at trauma is to see that the factors that play a role in the creation of memories are all at an extremely high level in a moment of trauma. Think about those in the building on 9/11. Their thinking had to be running wild with thoughts of escaping and the potential outcome. Emotions were coming out of fear and included terror, fear, anxiety, and depression among others. Every one of their senses was bombarded by a flood of data. The memory etched deeply into their brains in those moments. The triggers activate the brain to do something.

Addiction creates memories, mostly based on the reward system. We feel good, our thinking tells us it's ok to use, and most of the time the early memories of dependency are positive. Addicts build an internal database of those memories. They have a way of gleaning out and avoiding the negative memories associated with their using.

Some day they might be able to isolate a specific memory and erase it; right now we are nowhere close to that. We know that dependency on drugs can fundamentally change memories and at times erase them. Blackouts, when the body and brain are functioning but there is no memory of what happened, are an extreme example of this. What we can do with memory is to create new ones and to change the impact a specific memory has on our lives. We don't change the trauma; we change how we respond to the trauma. We don't change the memories associated with using or the triggers; we change how we respond to them.

To help someone in recovery we can:

1. Build positive memories that are built around their senses, thinking, and emotions. In DBT when they talk about emotion regulation, they use the acronym ABC. A is to accumulate positive emotional memories. B is to build mastery. The addict needs to understand that the disease can be mastered. They can regain control of their lives, but as is true with all new learning, it takes time, discipline and hard work. Take any one of those out and the odds of success go down significantly.

It is helpful in recovery to not only build mastery over the disease but also to find something else in life to master: an instrument, hobby, skill, exercise, or a wide variety of other things. Perhaps they used to have something they enjoyed but stopped once the dependency set in. Encourage them to rekindle that fire. The C is to cope, to think ahead and plan for moments you know will be difficult. The woman mentioned above came up with a strategy to go down the dairy/wine aisle. People who think and plan ahead do better than those who wing it—at least in addiction recovery. The more positive, creative, and healthy memories a person creates, the more likely they are to stay on that journey and not relapse. This holds true for depression as well, and many addicts struggle with depression.

   a. People like to tell their story. This is what step 1 of AA is about. If someone has been an addict for a period of time, the disease has become something they are familiar and comfortable with—a friend. When that person enters recovery, that friend needs to die. An integral part of death is grieving. It may seem odd that a person needs to grieve the loss of the addiction that was ruining their lives. Nonetheless, they have had a deep relationship with the disease; it has been an active and constant part of their lives. They are attached to that lifestyle. To think they can just move on without grieving is to miss something. A large part of the grieving process is to tell the story. Talk with them about that life; how can they describe the hole that is left by the disease being in remission? Those who report there are no holes (at least early in recovery) are either lying or avoiding reality. We need to remain non-judgmental when they do this. When we listen to a story we can hear and see how they react to what has happened, what the addiction has done for them and to them. What pieces of their life do they leave out? Why? Is there remorse, guilt, and/or shame? All of this takes time; it's an unfolding story. You will hear people's stories shift over time. New memories will surface, because they know in telling the story they help others as well as themselves.

2. If there are significant negative memories revolving around trauma, abuse, and/or grief, encourage them to find someone who specializes in those areas. If they don't those things are still in their brains and will still find a way to be pacified. Relapse is an easy option because it is what they know. Yes, going through the darkness that comes with those things is not fun, but neither is a life of addiction and avoidance.

Language—The main areas of the brain involved with processing language are **Wernicke** and **Broca**. Why is language important? Think of a world without any form of communication--how would you function? No written or spoken word, no sign language. If that were the case when you were born and raised, there would be little thought because thought is based on language. We would run primarily on instinct. Most animals have vocal or physical language they use for survival and courtship.

If we were to trace anyone's addiction to its origin, we would undoubtedly find language was there. Perhaps they were encouraged to use or read or saw something about the positive use of a medication or alcohol. When they started using, the reward system kicked in and mentally they told themselves this was a good thing. People with dependency issues use language to defend their behaviors; they use language with themselves and others to lie, cheat, and manipulate the world around them. When we do not have clear boundaries they will use language to move out of or around boundaries. For many addicts this process of how language can lead down the wrong path started in childhood. We find that most addicts have a great deal of shame in their lives. Shame, again, is the feeling that one is not worthy. When we hear those types of words we want to hide. There are a lot of ways people deal with shame in their lives; addiction is but one. What we hear, speak, read, or write matters. When we talk with addicts it's not about them being a bad person, it's about them making decisions and doing actions that are destroying themselves and the world around them. Guilt says, "I made a mistake. I'm sorry." Shame says, "I am a mistake."

Our culture is filled with language that glorifies using. People know where to go to be around people who have no problem with addiction—because they are often addicted. We all pick and choose what we listen to, read, say, and write. We make choices. In recovery the person needs to look at how language impacts their lives and change the pattern they have been used to. The language of recovery is fundamentally different than the language of addiction.

We can help the person in recovery by:

1. Watching their language. Listen to them speak, truly listen. Let them know what you hear them saying. The only way we truly know if we have been heard is to hear it back. Nodding our heads is not a true indication. If all they are saying is "life is great," something is wrong. Recovery is not a bed of roses 24/7. Encourage them to share their story, to write it down, to go and hear the stories of others as they do in AA. Encourage them to let you know when they are struggling, but we need to make sure we can be there for them when they need to talk or we will be telling them we aren't, which leads them to wonder why they are working so hard. It's not about you, but in their minds, especially in early recovery, to some degree it is.

2. Have them start keeping a journal. In the writings they can sometimes say things they are uncomfortable sharing with others. They can write their dreams down, which may give them insight. Over time the journal can show them how much progress they are making on all the fronts we have been discussing. Most journals are private; there is no expectation they will share it. There is a tendency when people write journals they know others will read to write differently, to be more cautious.

3. Find uplifting things to read or listen to. Music, movies, books, Ted talks (ted.com), YouTube, and spiritual groups are all places we can find language that makes us feel good or helps us grow in creative ways.

4. Sticky Notes—One of the greatest inventions of all time!!! Those who can see process up to 85% of the information we gather visually. We are amazingly good at pushing things down in our brains. This is much harder to do when it's right in front of you. Put sticky notes on the fridge, bathroom mirror, and other places the person in recovery frequents. Each time they see the note it will register in their brain and over time the impact can be significant. Depending on who they are, write things like: "You are special," "God loves you unconditionally," "You can do this—with help," "You have purpose." Of course the pronouns can change if they want to write them.

5. Be aware of what you say. Words are very powerful. This is not a call to lie--that only hurts-- but we can choose words of truth that speak to facts, care, and support rather than to criticism, judgment and shame.

We have looked at what goes on in the brain from a more scientific side, early warning signs that things are going the wrong direction in the brain, the change process and how to move ourselves or others between the stages, and at five parts of the brain and how they are impacted by addiction. Now we will look at three things that are very common among those with dependency issues and what can be done about them.

THINGS TO LOOK FOR

It would be wonderful if we had ways of identifying addiction before it reached that stage. Addiction can take years to fully bloom and most of us are too cautious to raise red flags too early. Sometimes caution signs can be helpful to the non-addicted, to catch themselves before becoming truly chemically dependent. Below is a list of a few things to watch for:

- They use more: instead of one drink they have three, instead of one pill they take two.
- They run out of medications faster.
- They become more avoidant and irritable—especially if they are "needing" the fix.
- They start to lose interest in activities—especially ones that have given their lives purpose in the past.
- They isolate—from friends, family, and those they live with.
- Their sleep cycles and eating habits change.
- They start taking more risks to use and while using.
- They get into legal trouble—DUIs, aggressive behaviors.
- Relationships start to fracture.
- Tolerance increases.
- Withdrawal symptoms increase and intensify.
- They use even though they admit it's a problem.
- Mood swings.

- Lack of motivation, increased procrastination.
- Blackouts, memory loss.
- Using in the morning.

The challenge is to be observant--stick to facts, not opinions. Don't judge the person, but report that behaviors associated with using are damaging their lives and yours. Addicts are brilliant at twisting things around because they have to convince themselves they are OK and can keep it going. Opinions are easy to deal with; facts are much harder. Two is better than one, five is better than two--as long as they have evidence that something is not right. Sharing how their using is impacting you is important. Remember, their brains are at war. Addiction is pulling them to use and the other part of their brain sees the destruction and wants to stop but has turned over control to the addiction. It is no more a matter of will than telling someone with the flu or cancer to fix it--now.

Addicts are often people of very strong will and are highly resourceful. Think about it: how much will does it take to consistently lie, cheat, steal, avoid reality, manipulate, and possibly work when you don't really want to and/or can't? It is a will that has turned against the person rather than trying to help the person. All of us need to have a significant reason to engage our will in order begin and maintain the change process.

The Change Process

One way of looking at this is through the **change process** used by Motivational Interviewing. They see change as a 5-7 step process, depending on which version you use. It's a helpful tool in knowing what stage the person you are concerned about or working with is in. Below are brief summaries of each step. You can find much more on the Internet or in books. Each of these stages engages different parts of the brain at different levels. To be in denial requires the brain to act differently than when it accepts reality. This does not excuse denial; it just helps understand it in a different light.

Precontemplation--This is where denial lives. Denial can exist both in the addict and in those around them. We don't want there to be a problem so we block out what is happening. Someone else may say something to us like, "Seems like Bill is having some issues with his drinking. Are you concerned?" If the person hearing that is in this stage they will respond by saying something like, "No, I think it's fine, he's always been like this, it's not out of control yet, I'm keeping an eye on it, mind your own business, thanks for pointing that out," etc., and then move quickly onto a different topic. The more defensive they become and the more readily they switch topics often serves as an indication of how deep they are into denial.

We don't move people from pre-contemplation by judging or being hyper-critical, but by sticking to the facts and offering to help when they need it. Don't ever offer to help someone if you don't mean it. They will use your failure to be there for them as evidence that there isn't really a problem after all. Do not challenge the resistance an addict puts up; roll with it. This may seem counter-intuitive but by doing so they do not perceive you as a threat and are more able to face the reality of whom they have become. We can help them see the specific problems dependency creates and allow them to develop internal motivation for recovery. Those who get sober for others do not do well.

Contemplation—Here, people have broken through denial and are thinking about where they have been and where they are going. They are facing reality, a key component of recovery. Addicts are on the run, often from many things, as we shall see in the next chapter. When they decide to stop running they need help to sort out fact from fiction and what to do about it. When people who live with and/or know someone with an addiction issue break through their denial, they too will need help as they move forward. An addict's entire system of life is impacted by their using; it's also impacted by their recovery. Many people who enter a treatment program have often broken through into the contemplative stage. They begin learning about what we are talking about in this book. They look at their lives and the habits they have formed. They start to learn coping skills that will help them ward off cravings and work on the different parts of the brain that have been hijacked. At this time they are just thinking about these things; they have not made a significant commitment to change. They may be in treatment because of pressure or to appease people rather than to fundamentally change their lives. Sometimes they underestimate addiction and feel now that they have broken through denial they have it all covered. It's a myth that people like being addicted; they just don't think they are or they don't see any way out.

For those who know someone who is addicted, denial is not that different. When they finally acknowledge there is a problem, they are often at a loss what to do about it. We can best help by getting them to people who work with addiction. There are strategies we know are more effective than others. If you are thinking of having heart surgery you don't ask your neighbor who is a landscaper or teacher, you ask a heart surgeon. Addiction is serious business and talking with people who understand it can save a lot of time, grief, and trouble.

Preparation—Now we are getting ready to act on the newfound beliefs. Everyone acknowledges there is an issue and everyone wants change. It's one thing to want change and another to move into the change we want to become. The addict's brain is going to fight change early in recovery; you/we need to be prepared for that. The dependent person's life has been revolving around that, often for years. Now they are going to stop. All the habits associated with the addiction are going to need to change. While their bodies will feel better almost every day for the first few months and their brains will function better, they are highly vulnerable to relapsing; don't be fooled. Relapse is amazingly easy to fall into. We don't think so because we want to believe that once denial has been broken through, no one would want to return to that life. They don't, but the reward pathway in their brain is entrenched and the person needs to cut a new reward pathway. To do that they need help, support, encouragement, and yes, at times a good kick in the rear. Preparation is about getting the ducks in a row. It is different for everyone. The best place to start is to look at the chapter on the Big 8 and look realistically at each item, seeing what the person has been doing and what they can do to improve each. In that chapter we will talk about goal setting. We don't want to set our goals or someone else's too high-- that usually leads to failure, which leads to relapse. Addiction loves failure; recovery loves success, even small ones. At the core of all preparedness is support. Who will be walking with the addict during this transitional phase into recovery? Are they part of a support group, be it an outpatient program or one of the 12-step programs? Do they have someone they can start to unpack their lives with? Who is going to hold them accountable and what will that look like? In our hospital we try to have as many of those things as possible lined up before a patient walks out the door. We like having "family meetings" to ensure everyone is on the same page. When a patient tells us they have it all covered and can do it on their own, we are confident we will be seeing them again. Can you fix a bad heart or kidney on your own? When you break a leg, can you take care of it all by yourself? Not well. In the best of times we are interdependent on one another for many things in life. Brutal independence is not healthy or helpful. Those who are successful in recovery learn they can't go through this alone.

Action--We are aware of the issue, we know what needs to be done, we have a system in place to help move into the doing stage. For many addicts this is a difficult stage. They are fine talking about change, but when it comes to actually living out the change they hit a wall. Because they have done any of the things they are planning, there is no reward, it's just what other people tell them will be a reward. We all know that exercise and eating well are good for us; we've never met a person who argues with that. So why don't we do it? In part because the reward is not evident in our brains. We like instant gratification. Those who enter recovery from any addiction basing that recovery on instant gratification will relapse. Yes, they do feel better, think more clearly, and believe they are fine. But the underlying issues that got them into this mess are probably still there, waiting. Recovery is about hard work that takes time. We can help the addict by letting them know this and helping them get busy re-organizing their brains and reward systems. Action is based on what we know helps the brain. The Big 8 is the best way to start that process.

Maintenance-- This stage focuses on long term recovery. It begins in addiction after around six months of significant change and no using. This is where we look at what it is going to take to maintain a life without using over the long haul. Assuming all is well when we are six months into recovery is insanity. Addiction is present for life. There is no cure; that is a myth. An alcoholic is one drink away from relapse from the day they stop drinking. That is how fragile they and the brain are. By continuing to be conscious of the Big 8 consistently, they can ward off most relapses. Many people in recovery stay in AA for the rest of their lives. Their brains are rewarded by the fellowship, sharing, camaraderie, and support they receive. We will not spend time on this because our primary concern is that first six months of recovery.

Relapse--The previous stages are part of the core theory; these next two have been added as people think and observe the process of change in people's lives. Some people believe that relapse is an automatic part of addiction. It is not. While it is true that a majority of addicts have a relapse in their lives and some have many, it is not a necessity. Relapse is a choice. A relapse triggers the old reward system with stunning speed. If we use the jungle metaphor, a relapse is like having 20 people with machetes and bulldozers at the edge of the jungle, where the old path started. It doesn't take long to clear the old path. Those who have been in remission for more than a decade usually return to the amount of their drug of choice where they left off within a very short time. The key in relapse is to catch it as fast as possible. People who stay in a sustained relapse struggle to regain their footing in recovery. Those who get help quickly (like within days or weeks) can often regroup well, see their mistakes and take steps to not repeat them. When you look at what and why someone relapsed, it usually revolves around an issue in the Big 8. They took their eye and brain off the work that needs to be done. Those associated with the addict need to be aware that relapse does happen. As we keep saying, judgment and criticism don't help. Understanding and support are important to the addict. They usually feel lots of guilt and shame for their relapse; they don't need others to be reminding them constantly of it. That just increases the amount of guilt and shame, further increasing the chance of ongoing use. Shame and guilt are two of the main foods of addiction; they want them to feel guilty. When dependent people have these feelings they will use in order to not feel them—the reward system in action again. The question should be, "Ok, you fell off the horse--why, and what are you going to do to get back on and stay on? How can I help?" This does not excuse the relapse; there are no excuses. This statement does say that you have some understanding of how difficult recovery is and you want to help them find sustained recovery.

At some point people have had enough. Ten to fifteen relapses is a bit much for many people impacted by them. Addicts burn bridges. You have the right to do that. Helping someone in and through recovery is not a right of the addict or an obligation of yours. It's a choice. We encourage people to never say never, but you may need some time. You may need a person to show you they are serious about recovery, and the best way to do that is by staying in remission. Addicts are not helped by open-ended commitments like, "Our relationship can get back on track after you have been in remission a while." What does that mean? A while can be a week, year, decade or never. Those helping addicts need to count the cost to them. Be as clear as you can within your own mind and to the addict as to the boundaries of your help. We all have them; make them conscious.

Read more on this in a wonderful book by Carlo DiClemente: **Addiction and Change: How addictions develop and addicted people recover**

Here is a bit more on relapse:

RELAPSE

While there is no hard and fast linear route to relapse, there are several things that tend to happen on the way. For those who are trying to help the person in recovery, we should not jump to conclusions and just assume they are in trouble. On the other hand, we all know that denial is part of the addictive mind, so we tread a fine line. Letting the person know what you see and that you are there to help if they want and/or need it is what is most useful.

For the first couple of months relapse is as much a physical condition as a mental. If they are doing the work of recovery, after six months it is virtually all mental. They relapse in their brains before actually using. There is no timetable for relapse. It can happen the day after sobriety begins or 30 years later. There is no timetable as to once this process starts how long it will take to relapse--it could be minutes, weeks or months. The time it takes usually shortens with each relapse. This is to say that the first time they may have some initial thoughts but can keep them at bay for a while. After several relapses the time between the initial thought and relapse is often short.

* Something in the person's life makes them not engage the process of recovery as well. It may be overconfidence or a stressor in their lives they are unable or unwilling to

deal with. Something may have happened that leads them to believe they can't do it, so why bother.

* They will ignore the warning signs they know exist and the reality of what they are doing or not doing—especially in relation to the Big 8.

* The lack of progress makes life uncomfortable. They start to exhibit behaviors like isolation, irritability and other coping skills that don't work and are common with the user. They will come up with "rational" reasons for all these behaviors—in their mind. Sometimes it is helpful to say, "John, if the roles were switched and you were sitting here watching me isolate, get irritable, and rationalize everything, what would you think or say?" Denial has crept in. This is not denial of using because they aren't doing that; it's denial that something is wrong or stressful in their lives they are having difficulty coping with.

* As they move closer to relapse, past triggers surface. They have been lying in wait. These will pull them closer to relapse or ignite it. The hope is they have a plan for all their triggers and use that plan. PAWS—Post-Acute Withdrawal Symptoms--also tend to show up at these times. Read the section on those. Routines in life are weakening.

* In early recovery the emotional center of the brain is highly vulnerable. The person will need to get used to emotions and learn to cope with them in positive and healthy ways. Historically they just used to cope with them. Emotions fester and deepen. Anxiety and depression increase and their willingness to face and deal with them decreases. They become increasingly defensive. Fewer and fewer activities related to recovery occur.

* The individual now feels overwhelmed and out of

control. They are quickly losing touch with the mechanisms available to them for recovery. The old reward pathway in the brain sounds easier and better at this time. They are not thinking past using to the consequences. The memory of what addiction did for them is increasing. In their mind options are running out. They see the choices they have as going insane, committing suicide, or using. They have no sense that they will be rewarded by pushing through it and asking for help. They become convinced no one will help them; they will only be judged. This raises the guilt and shame within them, which in turn adds to the stress within.

* The person often convinces themselves they can handle just one. By now they are avoiding help, not answering the phone or doing any activities that are consistent with recovery.

Here is the shortened version of what was just said about the process of relapse:

Change in Attitude
Elevated Stress
Reactivation of Denial
Recurrence of Post-Acute Withdrawal Symptoms
Behavior Change
Social Breakdown
Loss of Structure
Loss of Judgment
Loss of Control
Loss of Perceived Options
Relapse

People relapse; it's a fact. Addiction is a disease of choice, so they choose to relapse, but recovery is very, very difficult. How many of us get something right the first time we do it? Rarely. This is not an excuse, just an understanding. The people around the addict need to make up their minds what the boundaries are, to what extent you will hang in there through relapses. Just as we do not judge the addict, we do not judge those who have had enough.

Transcendence-- This stage discusses a time in the process of change where there is no going back. Think of learning a language. That change in learning and adapting to a new language is difficult, time consuming, and frustrating. There comes a time in that process where you no longer think in your native tongue and translate in your mind to the other, you simply live and breathe the new language. The same is true for learning a musical instrument. After a while you simply play; you don't have to think about it. The change is so deeply rooted in your being it becomes who you are at a core level.

Addicts can reach this stage of change where being in remission is such a part of their lives that using doesn't cross their mind. They know they can't use, they just don't need to put lots of time and energy into pushing those thoughts and cravings away because their brains have adapted to a new state of being and using is not part of that. The issues that got them into addiction no longer exist or have been dealt with. All the receptors are back to normal and the reward pathway has an extended life of new rewards. We call it transcendence because the person has transcended the change, no more change in that area is needed, and they are simply living the change, day in and day out. For true and significant change of any kind in our lives, this is where we would like to get.

This discussion started by talking about will. We need to assess where their willingness versus their willfulness are within each stage and which stage we are at in relation to the addict and where we think they are. Be honest and be open with yourself and others. If you aren't then you are still in denial at some level.

Where did all this start?

There is no line in the sand when someone passes from use to abuse to dependency. The nature of the disease is to fill life with shades of gray. Some people are able to catch themselves as they start to abuse substances or things and never become physically or psychologically dependent. The mechanism to enable that to happen is unknown. We do know that the vast majority of addicts have a least one of the following items in their lives, and many have all three.

1. **Genes**—While we have not pinpointed a location for the gene that predisposes a person to become dependent, few doubt there is a genetic component to addiction. This is not an excuse for the addict; it just means the slope is slipperier for them. Many people become addicted who have no history of it in their family tree and many people who have a lot of addiction in their family tree never acquire that disease. It does play a role.

Between 50 and 70% of those with addiction have it in their family tree.

At this time, there is nothing anyone can do about it. There is no gene therapy for addiction; it's just an understanding that it is probably there and the person needs to be careful. We encourage families to talk with their children (probably age 12-14) about this. Teens tend to see themselves as invincible, but at least they will have the information. Information, when used appropriately, can be invaluable. Gather information about your ancestors. Find out how widespread addiction is in the family tree. Remember that families are brilliant at covering up dependencies; they are often in denial. Encourage those with information to be honest; let them know it will help you.

People who are in recovery need to let their children and grandchildren know they probably have the gene and should be very cautious.

Again, having a genetic predisposition to addiction is not an excuse--it's still a disease of choice.

2. **Trauma/Abuse/Grief--**We talked in the last chapter about issues of trauma, abuse, or unresolved grief. Addiction can be a coping skill for the impact of these things in a person's life. Each of them impacts our brains in different ways. They influence our thinking, feeling, senses, memories, and language. They all cause internal pain to varying degrees. Most people do not like pain and we will

avoid it if we can. Addiction is a wonderful temporary avoidance mechanism. The problem is that while we are avoiding one (or more) issue(s) in our life by using, we create a variety of others. Pain that comes from trauma, abuse and/or significant losses doesn't just go away. These issues sit in our brain and want to be paid attention to. They may invade our sleep with nightmares or keep us from engaging in new relationships. We often hear of people that use to become less inhibited. They are socially cautious and using helps them to "lighten up." They are rewarded, as we have discussed, by their social interactions. The new normal revolves around who they are while using. Tolerance builds and addiction is not far behind. It would be much better to see what is behind the inhibition and work on that.

TRAUMA—First, a few statistics around trauma and addiction, related to alcohol, but similar statistics exist for other addictions:

- Between 25 and 75 percent of people who survive abuse and/or violent trauma develop issues related to alcohol abuse.
- Between 10 and 33 percent of survivors of accidents, illness or natural disasters report alcohol abuse.
- A diagnosis of PTSD (post-traumatic stress disorder) increases the risk of developing alcohol abuse.

- Male and female sexual abuse survivors experience a higher rate of alcohol and drug use disorders compared to those who have not survived such abuse.

Here is what is happening in the brain:

- The amygdala can become overactive. It is the emotional center of your brain that begins processing senses at an emotional level (fight, flight, and freeze). After a traumatic experience it is constantly on the alert for a new threat. It increases anxiety, fear and vulnerability. At the moment of the trauma it is on overload, helping to burn that particular memory deep into the brain.
- The hippocampus (your brain's center for processing memories) can become underactive. When this occurs, instead of moving a memory to passive long-term storage, the brain gets stuck in a memory loop—especially susceptible during sleep. Traumatic memories are around; they are triggered easily because of where they are stuck. The repetition of these thoughts, emotions, senses, and memories digs deeper into the memory base.
- The cortex (where thinking takes place) joins in. When a traumatic event is taking place, our survival skills take hold. Our lives depend on our survival; it is a critical function of being alive. When a perceived threat exists, everything else takes a back seat. Logic disappears and sometimes morals and ethics are diminished as well. Using becomes a way to calm the threat, to sleep

through the night terrors. At first people are often rewarded for their use; it does indeed give them a sense of temporary peace and calm. But trauma is more powerful than that. Like addiction, trauma is a force to be reckoned with. Even when you try to refrain from addictive behavior, you will experience an unstoppable urge to engage in it. Often when we feel a threat we want to run (flight). Addiction is running, and it doesn't work.

People with significant trauma want to feel safe and in control because that is what was lost in the midst of the trauma. Addiction can give the sense of feeling safe and in control—temporarily. There are other methods of increasing a sense of safety and control in one's life aside from using--methods that are more permanent, creative, and healthy. Here are a few areas of life as seen from an addictive perspective and from a recovery perspective.

- Being in control—As we said, those with trauma feel out of control and want to feel they have control of their environments. Using what they want when they want is a choice; it shows control. When they are addicted, they have lost control over it, over their brains, but the addiction convinces them they still have control (denial). Help the addicts find things in their lives they can control. The Big 8 are all things they have immense control over, so encourage them to focus on those. They can gain control over the impact of the trauma if they are willing to do the work, so encourage them to do so by letting them know you are with them as they go through it. Trauma work is very specific; it's much more than just having a chat about it. Most trauma survivors have done that numerous times and for many it ends up being a trigger rather than a help. To the degree possible, give them control. Along with this is creating a safe environment. Help the addict to talk about safety. People use to create a world of non-reality. It is a delusion of safety. What can they do in a non-using way to create an environment of safety? Addicts need to understand that the world is not going to change for them, but there may be some adaptations that you or others can make to help the person in recovery feel safer and in control without you having to give up much. There is no "entitlement" in recovery. Just because they have made poor decisions does not entitle them to demand what others do. Helping the person in recovery acquire new coping skills for moments of high stress or emotion can be invaluable. Here is a short list of coping strategies.

- Here are a couple of websites with lots of coping skills, including these:
- http://www.hubpages.com/health/Coping-Strategies-Skills-List-Positive-Negative-Anger-Anxiety-Depression-Copers
- http://www.yourlifeyourvoice.org/pages/tip-99-coping-skills.aspx
- http://www.beavercreek.k12.oh.us/Page/11 668

Diversions

1. Write, draw, paint, photography
2. Play an instrument, sing, dance, act
3. Take a shower or a bath
4. Garden
5. Take a walk or go for a drive
6. Watch television or a movie
7. Play a game
8. Go shopping
9. Clean or organize your environment
10. Read

Social/Interpersonal (with others)
1. Talk to someone you trust
2. If in a crisis, you can always call a crisis hotline
3. Set boundaries and say "no"
4. Write a note to someone you care about
5. Be assertive
6. Use humor
7. Spend time with friends and/or family
8. Serve someone in need
9. Care for or play with a pet
10. Encourage others

Cognitive (Of the Mind)
1. Make a gratitude list
2. Put sticky notes up with positive affirmations
3. Brainstorm solutions around what is causing the feelings or stress
4. Be realistic
5. Keep an inspirational quote with you
6. Be open-minded as long as recovery is the guide
7. Write a list of goals
8. Act opposite of negative feelings
9. Write a list of pros and cons for decisions

10. Reward or pamper yourself when successful
11. Write a list of strengths
12. Accept a challenge with a positive attitude

Tension Releasers
1. Exercise or play sports
2. Catharsis (yelling in the bathroom, punching a punching bag)
3. Cry
4. Laugh
5. Play music and dance
6. Play an instrument
7. Do something out of the ordinary that you don't usually do and is fun

Physical
1. Get enough sleep—7-9 hours per night; 6 hours straight if possible
2. Eat healthy foods
3. Get into a good routine
4. Eat a little chocolate
5. Limit caffeine
6. Deep/slow breathing
7. Exercise—minimum of 30 minutes cardio three times a week (consult doctor)
8. Stretch
9. Meditate with music

Spiritual
1. Pray and/or meditate
2. Enjoy nature
3. Serve others--get out of ourselves
4. Find a fellowship to join
5. Study—read something that will guide and support your spirituality

Limit Setting
1. Drop some involvement
2. Prioritize important tasks
3. Use assertive communication—be heard and listen
4. Schedule time for yourself

- Feeling hopeless, worthless, and having low self-esteem. Shame is very common among addicts and trauma survivors. When you have a self-image of worthlessness your brain wants to gather evidence to show you are right. They self-sabotage (including relapsing) life to prove their point. Every piece of evidence just shows they are worthless, so why bother. Being unable to "cope" with the trauma can get them started on this cycle, especially if they have had some of these ideas and feelings before the trauma. They may tell you that you are wrong or "you are just saying that" when you try to lift them up. They need to hear it nonetheless. We need to encourage and foster the person we know is in there, behind the trauma and the addiction. We don't approve poor behaviors and decisions, but we look for the wonder of the person and acknowledge that. We help the person look for ways of being successful because addiction loves failure. Small successes are important.
- Who are you? Who are they? Trauma and addiction impact how we see ourselves and how we relate to the world around us. Recovery means another readjustment in a positive and creative direction. We can help those in recovery by fostering positive self-image and direction. We can

67

validate the changes we see in them. This is strength-based work. It is not an avoidance of difficulties but a call to consciously look for and lift up that which builds a positive self-image. Many addicts over the years have lost a sense of who they are other than an addict. It is what their lives revolve around. That sense of identity does not change or go away overnight. Think about a doctor. Are they the same person and doctor the day they start as ten years later? We hope not. Experience and time matter. Time in recovery and a dedication to the recovery process matter, but recovery takes time, dedication, and patience.

- Soothe pain-- Without exception there is an underlying pain that comes with addiction, before, during, and after. If the person in recovery does not find a way to soothe that pain, they will probably relapse. The coping skills above, along with the Big 8, are wonderful ways to work with these concerns. Using and abusing medications and drugs is not an option.

- Memories—Trauma by definition brings up memories, uncomfortable memories. Addictions can help to push those memories down temporarily. We have not discovered a way to make memories disappear. We do not know which neuron(s) any given memory is attached to. What we can do is work on how much our lives are impacted by our memories. At some level we need to face the memories head-on. There are a variety of methods for doing this. We believe the research shows that EMDR (Eye Movement Desensitization

Reprocessing), EFT (Emotional Freedom Technique) and ETT (Emotional Transformation Therapy) are three of the best strategies to change the impact of memories. The key is to encourage the addict with trauma to get help to deal with the trauma and stop avoiding it. You can be very supportive and encouraging as they go through this difficult process. They will come out stronger, more resilient, and better able to stay in the course of recovery if they do.

Trauma needs to be taken very seriously. We all deal with trauma in different ways and we have yet to fully understand why that is. Certainly coping skills learned in childhood, our environment, mental and physical condition at the time of the trauma, type and intensity of the trauma, and how we are supported after the trauma all play a role. If a traumatic event is having a negative impact on someone's life, in this case the addict, then it needs to be dealt with. Help that person find someone who specializes in trauma and get the help they need. As is true with all things, trauma is not an excuse to use, it's a reason, and there are other ways of dealing with the trauma other than using.

ABUSE-- Abuse can be a form of trauma depending on its intensity and when it occurred. Traumatic abuse needs to be treated as trauma. Some people are in abusive relationships or situations while they are using. They may be using in order to cope with that situation which they see no way out of. It could be a relationship of codependency, or one in which they see no financial way out.

As is true with addiction, the person needs first to admit they are being abused. Denial can run as deep in trauma, abuse, and grief as it does in addiction. No one asks for trauma and no one wants to be abused. The challenge is how to respond to those in ways that are not self-destructive. Those working with the dependent person can help them acknowledge the abuse as well as the impact it is having on their lives—including their continued addiction.

Here are a few things to look for or to ask the person if they are seeing this in the relationship:

-Humiliation and put-downs
-Sarcasm
-Overly critical
-Won't talk and have a normal conversation
-Play the blame game; convince the person they are the reason for the abuse
-Jealousy
-Moodiness, especially quick shifts in mood
-Threats of leaving or pulling back
-Withholding affection—except after a significant event, when they may apologize and be affectionate
-Dominate and control

People in abusive relationships may make statements to themselves or others like:
"I know Jim doesn't mean it, he's just going through a rough time."
"I can't tell anyone because he will find out and get mad."
"I must have done something to deserve this."
"I can't ever do anything right with Joan."

"I feel so small when Dick does things like that."
"It's best to just keep quiet; things will settle down and be all right."
"Why can't I please him/her?"

There is no excuse for abuse--psychological, emotional, mental, or physical. None. If you are aware of someone in an abusive relationship we hope you will try to help them get help.

There are times when a dependent person will use in order to calm themselves instead of being abusive. At other times the use increases the abuse. Both are wrong and unacceptable. Those being abused need to be safe first and foremost. As is true with many reasons why people use, it may help cope with the abusive situation, an escape valve. Unfortunately it only increases the problems for the user and does nothing for the abuser.

We can help people in these relationships or situations by letting them know it is not about them. They too have shame and guilt and will be needing help to work through those issues. Their self-image has been damaged, which adds to the reason to use.

The skills mentioned above for trauma help with abuse as well.

GRIEF

All human beings have losses in their lives, from birth till death. We tend to think of grieving as only associated with significant losses through death. The grieving process is true for all losses and all people grieve differently; there is no right or wrong time frame or process. We do know there are parts of grieving that people go through and if they don't, they often pay a price for it, consciously or unconsciously.

Below is a brief description of the five stages of grief created by Dr. Elizabeth Kubler-Ross decades ago. It has stood the test of time and is a good vehicle to see how people are dealing with their losses.

One form of grief that is often not discussed is the loss of addiction. In true recovery, addicts are saying goodbye to their addiction--forever. Dependency has been their "friend," in some cases for a long time. They will feel it missing, which is part of what cravings are. Their lives for a time will not feel "normal." They get angry that they can't use anymore, they may be in denial that it's forever, they get depressed because of the early physical and psychological impact of recovery, and they may bargain with God or others to try to continue. This process is very normal in recovery, so be aware of it and sensitive to the person who is going through it, just as you would a person who has experienced a death.

Denial--Addicts are often the last people to know they have a problem. The brain is brilliant at rationalizing dependencies of all types. No one openly seeks to be an addict or wants to be one, so it's a natural progression of the disease to go through a period of denial. In the stages of change that we discussed earlier this is the stage of pre-contemplation--there is no problem. Even in early recovery people will still fight this. They may say on the surface that they are dependent, but deep down they are still in denial. The challenge for them is to speak the truth. Telling a lie only leads to guilt and shame, which leads to relapse. In order to help the person in recovery we need to help them feel comfortable being honest. If they choose to continue using, that is their choice and yes, it may have consequences. We do not judge the person, we simply hold people accountable for their actions. The addict has lost a sense of the person inside that wants recovery; we can help them re-find that person.

There is also often denial in early recovery that they are not well. They will look you in the eye and say everything is fine while the addiction is trying desperately to pull them back. People in the grieving process need to be authentic and make themselves vulnerable. In order to do that they need to be around people who accept them for who they are and walk with them through difficult times.

At times denial is a defense mechanism. Addiction uses it to keep the brain from facing reality. In recovery that is still there, along with the potential enormity of what has just taken place. In recovery we are talking about a systemic change that will impact every area of a person's life and all their relationships. That is a great deal to handle and denial is one mechanism to "protect" the person from the onslaught of that reality...which in the end they must accept to fully recover. One person said that denial is "the management of anxiety."

We can help the person get through this stage of grieving by:
-Giving them an environment where they feel they can be authentic and vulnerable without judgment
-Help them explore what it is they miss; hiding from those truths does not make them go away, exposing them takes away their power

-Let them know that you support them in their grieving and in their recovery.

-Get them to meetings where others are going through the same process or have been through it and understand it at a deeper level than you might. At 12-step meetings an addict can't say, "You don't understand," because they do.

-Part of the grieving process is retelling the story, again as they do in 12-step programs. Addicts need to look at the costs of their use as well as the rationalizations they used to use. They need to openly see and acknowledge how their brains have been hijacked.

Anger—We should not be surprised that someone in recovery gets frustrated or angry at this loss. After all, it consumed much of their lives. The lying, manipulating, hiding, rationalizing, cheating, stealing, avoiding, and denying took a great deal of time and energy for most people with dependency issues. If that is gone there will be some anger. Yes, they will hopefully understand it is truly for the best, but they are grieving a loss. The anger is at times irrational; such is the nature of the disease. They may lash out at people, blaming them for their condition. They may get angry at themselves for creating this reality. As long as the anger does not physically or emotionally damage others or property, it's fine; let them vent. We would be angry too if our lives were thrown into chaos and denial because of a disease we didn't see or understand that took control of our lives, especially when we have to accept full responsibility for allowing it to happen.

The addict has a choice. They can live in the anger and see how that works for them or they can choose to move through it and come out the other side to a new life, accepting the reality they have created and seeking to change it in the future. Those who are helping the person in recovery can help with this and all stages of grief. We can do that by:

-Letting them vent appropriately.

-If they are not showing any anger, ask them how they feel about the consequences of their addiction. This is not to be said judgmentally but in a way that helps them face the reality of their dependency and voice whatever is going on in their hearts and minds about that.

-This stage is about emotions, whatever they are. There is no timeframe for grieving and there is no linear path. Everyone grieves in their own way. When we feel we know how any given person should grieve, we are already slowing the process down. Do not confuse your grieving with that of the other. The reality is that at some level you are grieving too. This may seem odd to grieve the loss of addiction in another person, but it is what you have known and there are going to be changes because it is gone— hopefully mostly positive.

Retirement is a significant shift and loss in people's lives. We think that it should be all positive; you don't have to get up every day to go to work, no bosses, you can do what you want when you want, and a variety of other positive situations. But one day your life is filled with something that has guided you, perhaps for decades. Your work gave you meaning and purpose, relationships, exercised your body and mind, and paid the bills. In an instant that is gone. To think that is not a significant loss is naïve at best and can be dangerous. One of the largest "groups" of people who become dependent do so shortly after retirement. So just because we perceive things as changing for the better does not lessen the reality of the loss.

-Exercise is a great antidote for anger, especially when done with others.

-Creativity can be a wonderful outlet for anger. Writing, playing music, drawing, painting, or any other form of expressing what they are feeling in a creative way is useful.

-Perhaps getting them to take their anger and direct it toward something service oriented. We can counter emotions by doing the opposite (a DBT standard). Help them to help others, consciously moving out of the anger to do so.

Bargaining—We have all bargained. I will do X if Y will happen. "O God, I will go to church every Sunday if I can just have a drink." "I promise to not be abusive or drink too much if I can have just one." In recovery you are either all in or not. People talk about the harm-reduction philosophy, where we choose to reduce the harm by reducing the amount used. The problem is that if you are truly addicted it a) always comes with a cost, even if reduced, and b) doesn't work because of the nature of the disease. Harm-reduction is better than nothing and depending on the "reason" for use (i.e., opiates for true chronic and serious pain), it may be the best solution, but we should investigate this seriously and ensure the alternative of "no more" can't work.

We bargain because we don't like the new world order without what we have lost. Bargaining can offer us a temporary reprieve from the anxiety of the loss. We all need breaks in the grieving process; it's a heavy weight in

our minds and hearts. We like things as they were so we seek ways to get it back and mentally are willing to go to great lengths to do so, even if those lengths are lies or delusions. What you can do to help in this stage is:
-Don't offer false hopes. Don't buy into their bargaining. Recovery is recovery.
-Addicts need hope and you may be it. While there is no bargaining that is effective, we can offer hope about what life in recovery will bring.
-If you hear them bargaining don't be confrontational but try to help them see that it won't work, that it's not reality; it's yet another form of denial.
-Be thinking about what they are going to fill the hole that is left by not using with--what creative things can they do that will bring them purpose, meaning, hope, and a sense of value to themselves and those around them?

Depression—At some point grief hits us like a 2x4. We can become overwhelmed with the impact of the loss. Dependent people often have a period of depression in their life. We think they should be happy the disease is off their backs and part of them is, but the addiction is not happy with its demise. Remember, the brain is at war; addiction is still alive and well in early recovery and depression is a tool it can and will use to get the user to use. Depression leads to loss of hope and to isolation, two foods that feed addiction. Those around the person in recovery need to be as hopeful as possible and to not allow isolation to occur. This is another great reason to get them into a recovery program.

We can help most by not letting people in this stage of grieving get stuck, which is very easy to do. Addiction

77

knows this is a very vulnerable stage and it will do its best to get them to feel immense amounts of guilt, shame, blame, resentment, fear, doubt, loneliness, "woe is me," and a sense of alienation. This is fed by isolation. They will not be fun people to be around but if you can, be with them. You don't need to "do" anything. Let them exist in their depression and misery for a time. When they feel someone is truly there with and for them, they begin to let go of the depression because they see they have other resources to use. What we can do for people in the depressive stage of grieving is:

-Be with them

-Don't let them isolate or get stuck; get them out doing things

-If they get stuck help them seek help from someone who understands the grief process and can guide them through it.

-Sometimes people get really stuck in depression and may need some medicinal help. This is a temporary type of relief that gives their brain some relief and should only be used in conjunction with therapeutic help.

-If they are spiritually oriented, get them re-engaged with their spiritual foundations.

-Ensure they are getting enough (7-9 hours) sleep, but no more

-Exercise is critical; they need to be getting a half hour a day for at least the first 3 months

-Nutrition—What we eat matters and affects depression

Acceptance—Finally the person in recovery pops out the other end. They have accepted the reality of their disease and what the rest of their life will look like without addiction being an active part. They have hope and accept that staying well is their responsibility, with the help of others. They have found a new sense of life in recovery and have let the life of addiction move on. When they look back on the old life they do so with perspective. There is no denial of what happened, but the emphasis is on the here and now and a brighter tomorrow. All we need to do when someone is here is to be grateful, appreciative, and thankful to them for getting through it.

As has been said already, there is no set linear path to grieving and there is no set timeframe. Everyone is different. Some people will bounce around these stages for a long time till they finally reach deep acceptance. The challenge in recovery is to not get stuck. Grieving the loss of addiction in recovery should be a matter of weeks to months, as opposed to years. Being in grief is not an excuse to use or an excuse to isolate or be inert in life. Those are signs of being stuck and we can be most useful in pointing out they are stuck and letting them know we are there for them if they don't want to be in the relapse quagmire. We can only point out the behaviors we see and that there are consequences for those behaviors.

3. **Unmet Needs**—We all come into the world with needs, and from the second we are born till the day we die we have needs that are not fully met. A newborn needs air, sustenance and to be held, looked at and loved. To not have these leads minimally to significant difficulties later in life and potentially death. We know the damage of child abuse and negligence. Our needs in life ebb and

flow. Many know what it means to be healthy one moment and not the next, to have companionship and then to have that as an unmet need in our lives. We believe that one of the reasons people get into trouble with dependency issues as well as relapse with them is because of unmet needs. Dependency is a mechanism to cope with unmet needs at times. It is not a healthy strategy but it often works on the reward system. We hear people talk about "drowning my sorrow." They enter a mental state where the pain of the sorrow is given a reprieve. They are rewarded for that behavior—over and over and over. Addiction does not want the dependent person becoming aware and doing something about their unmet needs; they are prime fodder for the disease. To help someone in recovery, we need to find out what their unmet needs are and find creative and healthy ways of getting them met.

Whoever is reading this can do this exercise because we all have unmet needs. It's fascinating to see how we cope with those and which ones we tend to avoid. Avoiding a need always comes with a price.

Needs are those things that when absent have a significant impact on our lives. I can say I need a Lamborghini. We all know I don't. I fantasize or desire one, but I don't need one. With my current job and familial issues, I do need good transportation. If I don't have it I would have fundamentally shifted my life in ways that probably would not be possible and at least not beneficial. A basic care is more than sufficient. We are not against having things we want or desire, but when we don't get them they do not have the same impact as not getting what we need; that's the difference.

Below, make a list of what you think are your unmet needs. Ask the people you are working with in recovery what theirs are. When you have that list ask yourself what the impact is if you do not get it met. If the answer is nothing then it is not an unmet need. We encourage you to do this before you read on.

We have put together a list of needs based on Abraham Maslow's categories from the 1960s. We encourage you to make copies of this list. Put check marks by all needs that are all not currently met at a "C" level. Have the person in recovery do the same. We are trying to find out the needs that are impacting the disease and the potential for relapse.

Physiological Needs

Health

Sleep

To have food

Good nutrition

Exercise

To sleep peacefully

To be without pain

To have physical help

To be mentally stable

Relaxation

Safety Needs

To feel safe

To feel secure

To be safe from myself

Order

Stability

Consistency

Confidence

Emotional stability

Shelter

Belonging Needs

To belong to someone

To be part of a community

Intimacy—platonic

Intimacy-sexual

Companionship

To be trusted

To be able to trust

To be accepted

To accept others

To be appreciated

To appreciate others

To be respected

A sense of independence

To be reliable

To be able to rely on someone

To be honest

To not be lied to

Dignity

Integrity

To be transparent and open

To have affection

To give affection

To feel compassion

To matter

To nurture

To be nurtured

To be in partnership

To be a part of community

To hear

To be heard

To know

To be known

To be interdependent with others

To be in harmony with others

To be in
fellowship
with others
To feel
included
To give of
myself to
others
To receive
from others

**Self-Esteem
Needs**
To feel good
about myself
To have
purpose
To fulfill the
purposes I
have
To have a life
of meaning
To believe in
myself
Internal
balance
External
balance
Internal peace
External peace
Simplicity
Recreation

Curiosity
Achievement
Competence
Challenge
To be
effective
To grow
To learn
To be
passionate
To have fun
To have a
sense of
adventure
To laugh
To be
spontaneous

**Spiritual
Needs**
To feel
connected to
the
transcendent
To connect
with others on
a spiritual
level
To acquire
and maintain
spiritual

disciplines
such as:
  Prayer
  Meditation
  Study
  Fellowship
  Worship
  Service

Hopefully you and/or the person in recovery have some check marks. Ask the following questions:

1. Do you see how not getting that need more filled than it is can impact your life and potentially be a conscious or unconscious reason to use?
2. Do you see any needs that you checked that literally can never be filled? Not difficult or unlikely, but impossible. Why?
3. Do you feel someone is going to knock on your door and fill all those needs?

Now circle or designate three of the needs you wrote down or checked that if we could wave our magic wand, would be filled instantly. Which are the three most important unmet needs to get filled at this time in your life?

When you have done that, write down three things (for each need) you can do in the next month to get that need more fully met than it is today. Yes, we don't have a magic wand and no one is going to show up at your door-- unless you ask them to help. Needs get met when we become consciously aware of them and choose to do something about it.

We suggest using the SMARTS goal setting strategy when coming up with goals. Here is a brief description of the parts to consider.

S—Be Specific—Ensure that your goal is going to help get your need met. A goal of "running" is not very specific, "runs a marathon" is.

M-Measureable--We have asked you to write goals for the next month. Make sure an outsider would be able to tell if you (they) have been successful. If a person is serious about recovery, one of their goals needs to be to attend 12-step meetings of some type. To say attend meetings means technically that if you go to one meeting you have fulfilled your goal. We all know that one meeting in a month is not going to work. If you say you are going to exercise, walking around the block once is fulfilling that goal as written. A better goal is to cardiovascular exercise 30 minutes a day, four times a week. Ensure that whatever goal you set for yourself is measureable.

A—Attainable—Be realistic. Addiction loves failures. Recovery thrives on success, even small ones. Better to set your sight a bit low and be successful than too high and fail. You can always increase it in the future. Twelve-step programs talk about living one day at a time. Those who talk about being sober for the rest of their lives have already set themselves up to fail. Don't let them commit to 90 meetings in 90 days if it's not going to happen. The idea is that you are going to support them in these goals. Eternity is lived one day at a time.

R-Rational—Does what you say you are going to do make sense in light of the need you are trying to meet? If I state I want to run a marathon in a year, buying a car does not make sense as a goal.

T-Timely—For this exercise we set the time as a month. All goals have different time limits, but it's always helpful to have time limits on a goal so we know if we have achieved the goal or not. Many goals can be broken down into smaller goals. We are trying to help the person in recovery accumulate successes, the more the better. Each day of recovery is a success.

S—Support—Often we see the acronym as SMART goals. We believe that people who seek to do recovery on their own rarely succeed. How many serious diseases are "fixed" without help? We all need help in our lives. The person in recovery needs as much support as they can find, especially that first three to six months and if they surround themselves with good support during that time, they will not let it go after six months. Have them list the names and numbers of people they will share these goals with. Who are they willing to trust to encourage, support, and kick them in the rear to get the work done? It's one of the main jobs of being a sponsor in 12-step programs. We all need to be accountable. Thinking you can be accountable to yourself is often naïve. If that were true, the addict never would have become addicted. For those who have relapsed, ask them how being accountable to themselves worked for them. Support is critical and different areas of life need different types of support. Emotional, physical, therapeutic, spiritual, social, and mental support are each different, and no person can fill all those needs.

We have looked into some of the key reasons people become addicted or relapse. While there may be other reasons if we were able to isolate them, we feel the vast majority come down to the ones we have mentioned. Understanding how these are working in the lives of those in recovery is very important. How is that person dealing with the trauma, abuse, and/or grief in their lives? What unmet needs do they have? All addicts are running from something; it's important to figure out what that is and face it. Those things are not going away; they will lie in wait until an opportune time and then attack. It's better to get them off the table so they are not impacting those in recovery.

The Big 8

Recovery is at one and the same time simple, logical, and complex. What makes it complex is where addiction lives, the human brain. We all complicate our lives. We all know things we need to do that we don't. AA has an acronym, KISS: Keep It Simple Stupid. Simplicity and clarity highlight what needs to be done in any given situation, and recovery is no different. We have put together eight parts of our lives that impact dependency issues and life. If you look at people you would consider happy, they are at peace with themselves, motivated, healthy, and can cope with significant stressors in their lives in healthy ways. These eight things will be in their lives to a large degree.

Those in recovery need a course of action that is clear and can be accomplished without undue stress. Recovery is remarkably difficult. Addiction is not going away without a fight. Remember, their brain is still hijacked in early recovery and it is brilliant. The more of these eight things the person does, the faster the brain gets rewired. If they do nothing, the wiring does not change and they relapse. If someone relapses, go down this list and see what they were doing in each of these areas. The answer is probably not much.

While the person in recovery will need help in most if not all of these areas, you can't do it for them. The addict must decide to recover for themselves, and others will benefit from their recovery. When people get "sober" for others it doesn't work. You can't force purpose on someone, but you can help them find purpose and fulfill that purpose in their lives.

The goal is to understand each of these eight parts of life, to get the list on the refrigerator so it is consistently in our consciousness. Addiction wants this list in a drawer, out of reach, out of sight, out of mind. The person in recovery should try to do something in each category every day until it becomes a natural state of being. All of us should be doing these things, so as you are helping someone in recovery you might have the list on your refrigerator and be thinking about what areas need attention in your life. The Big 8 works with mental illness as well.

There is no order to the list; all are important. We are about progress, not perfection. The brain does not go from A to Z in a day. The idea is to see how these things can be worked on.

1. SLEEP:

Most humans sleep 1/3 of their lives!!! Think about it: if you live to be 90, 30 years of your life will have been spent asleep. There is a reason for this. If we didn't need it, the natural rhythms of our lives would change. Adults need 7-8 hours of sleep a night. Sleep goes in cycles of 1.5-2 hours. The human brain needs at least three of these cycles, preferably in a row. We know that sleep gives all parts of our brain a chance to relax, reorganize, consolidate memories, and secrete chemicals not done in a waking state, dream, and probably many others. We have learned a great deal about sleep in the last 15 years, and the more we learn the more we know we have to learn. Chemical dependency creates chaos in our biorhythms and sleep habits. When someone gets "used to" sleeping while under the influence, learning to sleep in recovery can be difficult. This is natural. If we do not get enough sleep, our brains are not at their full potential and in order to have the best chance at long term recovery, we need all the brain working at its best as much of the time as possible.

Make a list of things that currently get in the way of your sleeping well. The goal is to sleep well without the need for sleep aids, but sometimes those are necessary.

A few questions about your sleep habits:

1. On average, how many hours of sleep do you get a night? (Sober—sleeping under the influence does not count.)
2. Do you take naps? How long? (Naps can hinder a good night's rest.)
3. How many times do you wake up during the night? Is it always at the same time?
4. Do you know why you wake up?
5. What level of stress do you have in your life right now? (1-10)
6. Do you remember your dreams? (If you sleep more than an hour you dream, but you may not remember them.)

Why do we need sleep?

Our brains are active while we sleep; they are just active doing different things and at a different brain wave state. Certain chemicals are created during sleep that help us in our conscious time. We all know the feeling of being groggy, not able to focus or dozing off.

Below you can see typical graphs of what different brain waves look like and a common healthy sleep pattern.

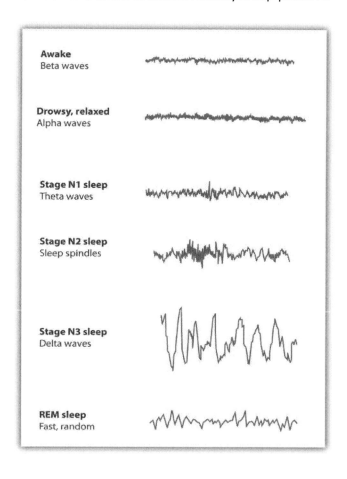

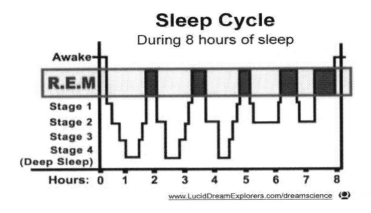

A very good overview of the impact of alcohol (and other drugs) can be found here: http://pubs.niaaa.nih.gov/publications/arh25-2/101-109.htm

Here are a few things we know happen during sleep. All of these are negatively impacted by addiction.

Helps consolidate information and make decisions. While we are sleeping, our brains are putting information together, processing it and preparing us to make decisions in the future. We gain insight during our rest. When we are not getting enough sleep, we take away this ability. It's like a librarian. If they are helping others all the time, there is no time to order books, shelve the books turned in or check out books for others. They need downtime for that, just as our brains need sleep.

Creates and consolidates memories. When we sleep we organize information we have gathered and we forge and deepen memory. Learning continues in our sleep. Sleep helps us lock in new learning and memories. As you are creating new memories in recovery, good sleep habits will help them become more locked in. We have learned that the ability to remember new information is hindered up to 40% by lack of good sleep. Do you want the new you being created to be hindered that much?

Makes creative connections. Creativity itself is helped in and through good sleep. Recovery takes creativity. You can't keep doing the same things; life needs to change. It will take creative energy to find ways of organizing your life around habits that build self-esteem, stability, consistency, purpose, health, and good relationships. Giving your brain a good rest gives it the increased capacity to do that.

Clears out toxins. During our waking hours toxins can build up in our brains and bodies. Sleep gives the brain a chance to do some basic cleaning. Physically we are creating some positive and necessary chemicals, while breaking down and getting rid of others. As we start to forge poor sleep habits these same toxins increase, impacting our brain functions.

Using before sleep may create drowsiness because it increases melatonin production and relaxes muscles, but when sleep happens, the destructive nature of the substances continues, adding toxins to the bloodstream and brain, inhibiting the repair work that takes place during sleep and slowing down the processing speed to reorganize information and consolidate memories. As we habituate this process, the brain habituates that neural pathway, making it difficult to change—but it can.

Learns and remembers how to perform physical tasks. Part of dream sleep (REM) is turning short-term memories into long-term ones. When we have poor sleep, our memories do not form as well, clearly, or deeply. Things we learn how to do physically during our waking hours become more deeply embedded in our sleeping hours.

We do not fully understand REM sleep other than to know it is a necessary part of sleep. Animals that are deprived of REM sleep become "psychotic" within days and die within weeks. Humans who do not sleep (for any reason) also have hallucinations, become psychotic and eventually decompensate. While we may believe dreams are meaningful on a different level, there is no doubt that REM sleep is a critical part of our overall sleep cycle—whether we remember them or not. Addiction inhibits REM sleep; it narrows the amount of time spent in REM sleep and decreases production of neurotransmitters (especially GABA).

HOW TO IMPROVE SLEEP

- Set a schedule: Sleep is a habit. When you go to sleep, where you sleep, how you get to sleep and how you wake up are all parts of the process. Go to bed at a set time each night and get up at the same time each morning. Don't take naps. When we nap, we rarely get a complete sleep cycle. Lots of 30 minute naps do not add up to a good 6 hours straight. For one, you will not get REM sleep if you only sleep 30 minutes. You will sleep better without naps. Exercise: Try to exercise 20 to 30 minutes a day. We know how important exercise is to life in general, but those who regularly exercise sleep better, have few cravings, less anxiety and depression, and feel more balanced. More on this in the next section.

- Avoid caffeine; it's a stimulant. Smokers can go through nicotine withdrawal during sleep and wake up to curb the cravings and withdrawal symptoms. Alcohol inhibits REM sleep and keeps people in a very light stage of sleep, the brain still highly active. Many people, especially those over 50, should avoid drinking liquids more than two hours before bedtime because they will have to get up to empty their bladder.

- Relax before bed: Sleep is a habit. Create habits that help you fall into a relaxing sleep. Listen to pleasant music, take a warm bath. Associate certain activities with sleep, including where you do it. Build a habit that bed is for sleep, chairs are for focused reading and work. Most people do not sleep well going to sleep with TV or music on or having the glow-in-the-dark clock looking at them.

- Sleep until sunlight: When possible wake up in the morning. Our biorhythms are not meant to go to bed at 1 am and get up at 11 am. Sunlight gets our biorhythms in sync; it starts an internal clock. If you work nights, your body will adjust to that schedule, but going back and forth is difficult for the brain.

- Don't lie in bed awake: Insomnia leads to insomnia. Do something that will relax you or tire you out if you are physically not tired. If this is a regular pattern, you are probably not eating well or exercising enough.
- Control your room temperature: A room that is too hot or too cold may inhibit sleep. Everyone's needs are different but be aware that temperature, as well as stale air, does impact sleep.
- See a doctor if your sleeping problem continues: If you try these things and still have a hard time getting to sleep or staying asleep consult a doctor or a sleep specialist. There are sleep disorders, many of which can be treated. Sometimes sleep medications are needed to help create a new sleep habit.

This process is about building a new habit, a new way you sleep. It takes time and will come with some frustration, so be patient but diligent. The rewards are immense for life and recovery.

2. EXERCISE

Exercise is another critical part of recovery. Exercise gives your body what it needs to repair itself and to continue growing. Our brains are the center of issues with addiction and mental illness. The food your brain cannot live without for more than a few minutes is oxygen. Most of us take in far less oxygen than we can and should.

Exercise forces us to take in more oxygen and our brains are thankful for it. As you can see below, exercise helps many parts of the brain affiliated with chemical dependency.

- The prefrontal cortex is our thinking brain. Lack of exercise and oxygen impair memory, behavioral control, decision-making, flexibility, and thought cycles that lead to depression and addiction.
- Nucleus accumbens—associated with the reward system in the brain; positive reinforcement associated with addiction
- Hippocampus--high association with memory, especially declarative and spatial, which are part of the depressive cycle
- Amygdala—One of the emotional centers. Increased exercise leads to a more heightened and realistic sense of the fight, flight, or freeze response and the emotions surrounding those.
- Thalamus—Our thalamus is the gateway to the brain of our 5 senses (other than smell). Memories and thoughts come from our senses. Because our senses are wired and experienced through our brain, exercise impacts how that information is transferred.

Regular exercise has been proven to:

- Reduce stress-- Exercise has been shown to alleviate physical and psychological stress. The endorphins released and the distractions from the stress both play a role in that.

- Ward off <u>anxiety</u> and feelings of <u>depression</u>-- We have already discussed the reward cycle and how it inhibits the production of dopamine, a necessary neurotransmitter to help us feel good. People replace the dopamine with alcohol and drugs. The dopamine machine stops because it's not needed. Now that the person has stopped using they need to get the dopamine machine working again, the faster the better. Exercise creates natural endorphins that help that process.
- Boost self-esteem—The Mayo Clinic tells us that exercise is "meditation in motion." Exercise gives our minds a break from the stressors in life and the increased oxygen allows our brains to do necessary repair work and process reality better. Chemical dependency does not want this to happen; it wants the brain functioning at the lowest level possible.
- Improve sleep
- Ward off cravings and increase resiliency—Exercise creates a new way to feel good about ourselves; it gives the brain the main food it needs, oxygen, and creates a new pathway in the brain to get rewarded rather than the destructive path of addiction.

Exercise also has these added health benefits:

- It strengthens your heart, increases energy levels, lowers blood pressure, improves muscle tone and strength, strengthens and builds bones, and helps reduce body fat.

Below is an exercise inventory. It's a good, basic way to look at your life or the life of someone in recovery and see the impact of addiction and exercise. Doing this every few months can be helpful for all of us. It should go without saying that in recovery, honesty is critical. When those in recovery start misrepresenting the truth to others, they do so to themselves as well. Relapse is not far behind.

Exercise Addiction Inventory

The Exercise Addiction Inventory (EAI) (A. Terry *et al.*, 2003)

	Strongly disagree		Neither agree nor disagree		Strongly agree
Exercise is the most important thing in my life.	1	2	3	4	5
Conflicts have arisen between me and my family and/or my partner about the amount of exercise I do.	1	2	3	4	5
I use exercise as a way of changing my mood (e.g. to get a buzz, to escape etc.)	1	2	3	4	5
Over time I have increased the amount of exercise I do in a	1	2	3	4	5

day.

If I have to miss an
exercise session I feel ○ 1 ○ 2 ○ 3 ○ 4 ○ 5
moody and irritable.

If I cut down the
amount of exercise I
do, and then start ○ 1 ○ 2 ○ 3 ○ 4 ○ 5
again, I always end up
exercising as often as
I did before.

Note: We do not believe that exercise needs to be the most important thing in our lives, but we do know that a life without exercise is never fully lived.

HOW MUCH EXERCISE SHOULD I DO?

First, how many hours a week do you exercise--heart pumping exercise? Be honest!!!

The answer to how much is you probably need to do more, unless you are already doing 30 minutes per day or more. That should be the goal—30 minutes, at least 5 out of 7 days a week. Your brain and body will applaud you and you will feel the difference.

What kind of exercise should I do? We do not want to further damage parts of our bodies that are already severely impaired. The only reason to not exercise vigorously is because your doctor tells you not to. These exceptions are extremely rare. We can all find many

99

excuses to not exercise, and those with chemical dependency issues can find even more.

Asking a doctor or a trainer for suggestions is the best. Start slow. If you haven't been exercising, a good 15-minute walk would be great. Set yourself some goals (which you share with someone else for accountability—or that they share with you if you are helping someone in recovery) and stick to them. Build up slowly but surely. Walking, biking, swimming, the gym, running, and many others are all good. Get the heart pounding!!! Feed the brain the oxygen it so yearns for.

None of these eight things are rocket science. We all know what exercise is and we know if we are doing enough. The challenge is not in understanding what to do, but getting ourselves and others to do it. The motivation in addiction is the phenomenally powerful impact on the brain, body, and resiliency that comes with it.

3. NUTRITION

Nutrition is vastly underrated in terms of addiction, anxiety, depression, and mental illnesses. Think about it this way: what we put in our mouths ends up in one form or another in our brains. Do you want your brain running on beer and donuts? We all know that the American diet is filled with additives, fast food, and sugar. This is not a call to a radical diet, it is a call to look at what you eat and what, realistically, you can change. Some people will claim it costs too much to eat well: that is an excuse.

Neuroscience is learning how interconnected our diet and our thinking, learning, emotions, and behaviors are.

Most people know what foods are good to eat and which are not. The challenge is getting ourselves to eat well rather than knowing what to eat. Like chemical dependency, we have trained our brains to enjoy certain foods that are not good for us. We have to put in the time and energy to retrain the brain.

Food supplements can help, and we encourage a once a day vitamin to fill in some of the gaps, but supplements are not the same as eating a balanced, nutritional diet. Below are a few basics. As with all things, we encourage a visit with a doctor or nutritionist. The person in recovery needs to let them know they are in recovery—it makes a difference.

Most people who are using or are in the midst of a period of imbalance have significant deficiencies of nutrients. As is true with most things in life, MODERATION. We are seeking to have a healthy, balanced diet. There are times when our diets need to change due to illness or imbalance. Consulting a doctor or nutritionist is the best advice.

CARBOHYDRATES-- Good carbs, known as complex carbs, include potatoes, whole wheat bread, rice, cream of wheat/oatmeal, high fiber cereals, whole grain pasta, fruits, and vegetables. Good sources of fibrous carbs include beans and asparagus, among many others. Carbohydrates break down and not only give us energy, but trigger insulin production that helps tryptophan enter the brain. This helps with the production of neurotransmitters that help with depression and anxiety. Those with very low carbohydrate diets have less tryptophan and serotonin and become depressed and anxious more readily, which can lead to a relapse.

PROTEINS—Proteins are made up of amino acids. Twelve amino acids are made inside our bodies. There are eight that have to be supplied through diet. A good protein diet supplies all of these. Milk and other dairy products (including eggs) and meat are high sources of protein. Soybeans, lentils, peas, broccoli, asparagus, and seeds are all good sources of protein in vegetables. Proteins are the building blocks of who we are. Protein-deficient people do not do well.

Dopamine is made from amino acids. This neurotransmitter, along with tryptophan, plays a critical role in having a balanced mood and a sense of calm.

ESSENTIAL FATTY ACIDS—A significant part of our brains is made of fatty acids. We read a lot about Omega 3 and 6 fatty acids. They are a key ingredient of membranes in our cells. What do you think happens when the cell walls of your brain are weak? A significant lack of Omega 3 fatty acids leads to disturbances of neural functioning. Foods rich in Omega 3 and 6 include fish, broccoli, kale, spinach, seeds, peanut butter, and eggs. Today you will find many foods are enriched with Omega 3. You can also take Omega 3 supplements.

VITAMINS and MINERALS—There are a lot of types of vitamins. The ones listed below have an impact on addiction and mental illness more than others. Taking a once-daily vitamin often takes care of day-to-day deficiencies but is not a replacement for a well-balanced diet. B2 and B6 are associated with depression (vegetables, fish, chicken, pork, breads). B12 impacts our thinking patterns. Vitamin B complex also seems to impact dreaming and dream memory (fish, some cheeses, meats, eggs, food fortified with B12). Folate, more commonly known as folic acid, is associated with depression and its symptoms (lentils; dried beans and peas; dark green vegetables such as broccoli, spinach, collard or turnip greens, okra, and asparagus; and citrus fruit and juice). Having a balance of calcium, chromium, iodine, iron, lithium, selenium, and zinc also helps balance the overall system. All of these are found in meats and vegetables and can be supplemented with once a day vitamins.

Again, remember that BALANCE and MODERATION are what we need to seek. Deficiencies and excess can both lead to unpleasant consequences and interfere with long-term recovery.

We can learn how to do many of these eight things at the same time if we are creative. Go for a brisk walk to the store. Buy good nutritious food, walk home, cook a great meal and share it with friends!!! Exercise, nutrition, connection, fun, unmet needs, purpose, and spirituality could all be part of that.

Begin to rid the residence of the person in recovery of "bad" foods. It's important to not only get rid of the substances but other things that will potentially lead to relapse. Start to fill the residence with healthy things to smell, see, hear, taste, and touch.

4. HAVING FUN

Having fun is an important part of life. When is the last time you/they truly had fun? Sober. Mental illness and chemical dependency squash the brain's ability to enjoy life. Addiction fools us into thinking we are having fun, but we all know it's not fully real. Read the section on the brain to understand why this is.

We build habits in our brains as to what fun is and what is fun. That is why sewing is fun for some people and not for others. Below are some websites with lists of some things people find fun. Print a list and put a check mark by everything on the list you think is fun that you either have not done or have not done sober in the last three months. Then circle four of those things you can do in the next month. Feel free to add other ones that you enjoy that aren't on the list!!! You can always just write down a list of 20-30 things that are fun for you or that you would like to try that seem like they should be fun.

If you have not had fun in the last few months you will need to retrain your brain as to what it means to have fun. Some of the things you know used to be fun may not seem fun the first few times you do them. It takes the brain three to six months to get back on board, to get all the neurotransmitters functioning again, and they are what make us feel "good."

There is no right or wrong way to have fun as long as it is healthy and helps recovery, not relapse.

http://www.thesimpledollar.com/100-things-to-do-during-a-money-free-weekend/

http://www.wisebread.com/50-ways-to-have-free-outdoor-fun

5. CONNECTIONS

The human brain is hard-wired for connections, relationships.   Some of us are more introverted and prefer being alone than with other people. While this is normal, introverts need to push themselves to make connections with others, just as extroverts need to learn to spend time and be comfortable with themselves.

The types of connections we are talking about are face-to-face connections with other people. Pets are fantastic, but they can't replace what human interactions do in the brain. Neither can phone calls, texting, or chatting on line.

It's one of many reasons outpatient groups, therapy groups, and AA work. They are meant to be places where we feel more comfortable because there are others there in similar situations, people going through the same things.

One of the key purposes of connecting is to gain support for the life we are trying to build and live. They are hopefully also relationships and places where we can feel safe being vulnerable, sharing with someone or others about our struggles--a place where we don't worry about lowering our pride. Do you have people or places where you feel you can truly do that? For example, someone or some place you can go to when you are having cravings, are highly anxious, feel you are heading in the wrong direction or are starting to get depressed? List them.

Are you a person that the one in recovery can come to for support? Can they make themselves vulnerable without judgment or criticism? This does not mean we roll over and let them walk on us or abuse the relationship. This gets back to boundaries that need to be clear. But before you start working with someone in recovery you need to check yourself and see if you are ready. Their needs and yours may be different—probably are. What enabling behaviors have you had in the past and what have you done about them? Do you have someone you can turn to if and when things get difficult?

An excellent, if not a bit technical, article by Dr. Daniel Siegel, http://www.communityofmindfulparenting.com/curriculum/week2/S2-Article-InterpersonalNuerobiology_DanSiegel_EntireArticle.pdf, can shed some light on the importance of relationships and attachment. One of the points Dr. Siegel makes is about how relationships help the brain. While his focus is primarily on infancy and childhood, we believe these same five ideas are critical in having a secure relationship in recovery.

1. Collaboration-- The human brain likes to connect and collaborate. We are not created to be alone. Those in recovery deeply need to collaborate with others--for support, accountability, ideas,

encouragement, and sometimes a good kick in the rear. True collaboration comes with truly hearing and being heard. Those are built upon trust and respect, which is often missing in the early stages of recovery. We encourage those helping to find common ground where you can collaborate. That person needs to give as well as to receive. Collaboration includes brainstorming around the Big 8 and obstacles to success. It involves us sharing our struggles as we help them with theirs. This is not a 50/50 proposition, but one that we enter knowing that at times our vulnerability helps the person in recovery become more vulnerable.

True collaboration is founded on empathy, the antidote to shame, which most addicts have a large amount of. Empathy finds the wonder within each person while not excusing the bad behaviors. Empathy breeds hope and calls out the person that has sometimes become lost in the chaos of addiction. Empathy is not a doormat but can be a balancing bar as the person in recovery walks the tightrope.

There are many things in recovery that are not black and white. Not using is perhaps the one black and white issue. There are many things the person in recovery probably shouldn't do or think about, but creating an environment where it is OK to do so, to broach the subject, can be very healing. As we collaborate we help our brains and make more dopamine, serotonin, and oxytocin, all of which lead to stronger, healthier brains.

2. Reflective Dialogue-- All of us have "states of mind," which can include emotions, thoughts, memories, ideas, values, beliefs, opinions, and attitudes. The addict's brain has created a large amount of all those, most of them based a misinterpretation of reality. It is through reflective dialogue that the addict reorients to reality and dispels the myths. One example of this may help. Many chemically dependent people will think to themselves after six months of sobriety, I'm fine, I've been clean six months, they told me my brain would be "back." *It is; I think I can handle one.* They don't bother to share this with anyone that understands addiction because they know what the answer would be: "Are you crazy?!!" This is where reflective dialogue can be very beneficial. Here we are trying to bring meaning into life. This is not a time to tell, but to dialogue. We all know that insights we come to ourselves are more deeply embedded in our brains than if we are just told. Help the person to gain insight through questions and dialogue rather than "I know the answer, just listen." Chemically dependent people have amazing minds. They understand and see things in remarkable ways when they are thinking clearly. We can all learn from them. All of us need a check and balance to our brains. We get into trouble when we truly believe everything we think is true.

Dialogue at this level is a journey of exploration. What are they learning about their dependency? What are they learning in recovery? What is bringing meaning to their lives? Are there obstacles in the way? Which of the Big 8 are the most problematic at this time? While working on your relationship with the person in recovery, you can be of immense help looking at their other relationships--past, present and future. You are not a therapist, but you can have some very good conversations. There are relationships they will need to leave in the past or they will get dragged back into the pit. There are some that can be repaired--over time. The addict must be patient; trust and respect take time and are earned. For many there are relationships where the bridge is gone and will not be coming back. At some point they may need to face that reality and move on, as painful as it is. They may be the one that blew the bridge up.

Relationships are what the human dynamic is based on. Without them there is little to nothing. We all start somewhere and there are a wide variety of places anyone can find a relationship. AA, church, hobby groups, and support groups are but a few. Encourage them to build more relationships with others. If you are the only person in their life it puts a lot of pressure on you that you don't need. It breeds co-dependency, which is unhealthy for all involved.

The dialogue here is reflective; reflective in a secure setting where respect and trust hold forth. This does not mean their ideas and thoughts can't be challenged, but the challenge comes out of a deep concern for them, not out of judgment.

3. Repair—Let's be real, at times relationships are not perfect; they fracture. You or the other person says something, perhaps something vastly misinterpreted, and that strains the relationship. At times the person in recovery, especially as they get closer to relapsing, will self-sabotage a relationship. At that time you will have a decision to make. We cannot pursue those in recovery across the universe, which is enabling. We can let them know we are there for them in sobriety and can work through things if they are willing to do so. We can never do more work than they are. If we are working harder on their sobriety than they are, they will relapse. We can be there for them.

There is no magic number as to "how many chances" we give someone. That is up to you. If you feel guilty for not helping more, then you need to get some help. We are all not much help to others if we don't take care of ourselves. We tell addicts they need to put their sobriety first. You need to put your balance and wellbeing first. Now may not be a good time for you to help someone in recovery; that is OK.

Repair comes most smoothly and quickly when there is open dialogue and a lack of judgment. Pride and shame are the friends of addiction and the enemies of recovery.

We can help repair before the damage is even done by being dependable, consistent, predictable, intentional, and mindfully caring.

4. Coherent narrative-- All of us have stories. Our stories come from how we have perceived the life we have lived, starting in infancy. The person in recovery needs to figure out their story, part of which will probably not be very positive. We are not here to make everything a bed of roses. Reality needs to be faced. But stories can change; new chapters can be written. AA is filled with people who have made a choice to do that and to share the old story with the new. Some addicts will fixate on the past, struggling to let go of either the damage they have done or the resentments they carry with them. Both lead to relapse. Telling the story is important, but so is moving on. How can we help them build an honest story that acknowledges the past, owns it, but states, "It's not the end of the book?" This goes along with steps 4 and 5 in AA. They speak of the damage and impact of addiction and they make amends when possible, but sometimes it isn't. What can they learn from their story? What parts are they ignoring (both positive and negative)? At times the most important parts of the story are the ones left out the first go-round. In our hospital people complete step 1, their story. It is no surprise that when people relapse and return and do it again that the story changes. One part of their life will not be as

important or significant and another will rise to take its place.

Everyone has a story—help them to tell it and make sense of it. One of the things we look for in the telling of stories is ownership. Do they own their lives or do they play the blame game—which always leads to relapse. People in recovery know what we want to hear. We have to be cautious to not put words in their mouths and to validate (not agree with) what they say. In so doing they become more comfortable being vulnerable and speaking their truth rather than yours. Listen for signs of hope and support those. When we hear no hope, relapse has probably found a foothold in their mind already. Depending on how well you know them, you may be able to help them find pieces of hope.

5. Emotional communication-- While much of the above revolves around more mental communication, all humans are emotional. We can pretend that is not true. We can ignore our amygdala and other emotional centers of the brain, but we do so at our peril, as an addict or not. The brain functions as a single unit; we don't turn parts of it off and on at will. When we suppress parts, it impacts the others. Those who purport to not have emotions will undoubtedly have issues in other parts of their brains and lives.

Most chemically dependent people have extremes when it comes to emotions. They either have highly exaggerated ones (get very depressed, angry, and anxious) or their emotions are flat-lined; they bury them because they are too difficult to face and the substance helps that happen. Emotions stagnate in addiction. As with many things in life, the person in recovery will need to relearn how to be in touch with and manifest their emotional state. You can help by a) being aware of this reality (they may seem emotionally immature, b) encouraging them to be open and honest about what they are feeling, and c) being open and honest about what is going on inside of you. This is especially true when it comes to difficult emotions. Don't forget, their addiction is fighting for its life in their brains and emotions are one of the many tools it will try to use to get them back. By ignoring emotions they simply give that part of their brain over to the addiction. It doesn't take that many parts of the brain to be back in the addiction camp to lead to relapse.

We should not be surprised to discover that many people (especially those who were addicted at a young age) were missing some or all of these components of good communications with those around them, especially the adults.

Take a look at your own relationships. How do they stack up in reference to these issues? Ask the person you are helping who they have in their lives that give them these things--probably few.

When all of these things are working in a relationship, every part of the brain we have discussed that is hijacked by addiction is fed in healthy ways. We think and feel better, we express ourselves in more effective ways and our lives are more filled with meaning and purpose.

How many people do we need in our lives? There is no magic number, but seeking at least three to five is a good place to start. It is very normal to need help in life; everybody does. Those who convince themselves they need no one are in denial of the biology of the human brain.

Let's assume for a moment that you (they) don't have anyone on the list or that there are only one or two. Where can we find good, positive, supportive people? Of course, we don't build a deep level of trust the first time we meet someone, but as we expose ourselves and feel they are exposing themselves, trust is built. People will probably not break your door down to build a relationship; we need to often take the first step. You might be the person to let someone in recovery know you are there for them.

Here are a few places where you (they) should be able to find people to connect with:

a... Outpatient programs around the issue that you are coming to grips with
b... AA or other 12-step programs
c... Recovery groups-- Depression, Grief support groups (NAMI is a good source)
d... Churches, temples or other spiritually oriented places
e... Hobby groups (look at meetup.com for a long list of "groups" around a variety of things)

f... Therapists—Therapists can be a wonderful support, especially in early recovery; they can also be a source of encouragement and accountability as you seek to broaden your support network
g... Can you think of others? List them.

See if the person in recovery can list some people they would call if they get in trouble. Let the person in recovery know the importance of having people in their lives:

-Help them know they are not alone
-Give them a place to vent
-Help them build and solidify skills needed to stay balanced
-Give them the opportunity to learn how to build meaningful relationships
-Can act as a place to try out ideas they are having
-Are great brain food
-Challenge their behaviors and thoughts in constructive ways
-Give them an opportunity to share their insights and skills with others
-Teach them the benefit of being vulnerable
-Can reduce their shame and guilt
-Build self-respect
-Act as a source of accountability
-Share struggles around boundaries, sleep, exercise,
  nutrition, triggers, stressors, and find some
  potential resolution to those struggles.

It is suggested (wisely so) that those in recovery not enter into romantic relationships for a year. If they are in a relationship already, of course, we are not encouraging getting out of it. Here are a few things to consider about being in a relationship with a recovering addict.

An important axiom for those in relationship with an addict: "I didn't cause it, I can't control it, and I can't cure it."

1. **We all have baggage and addicts bring that with them into the relationship.** Being in a relationship with someone in recovery means hearing and understanding their story. This need not be a daily occurrence, but the disease is no different than any other disease. Significant others need to know about it and its impact on the one in recovery. Some people in recovery will wait a long time to tell the other person about their addiction. This is not a good sign; beware.

2. **One is too many.** If someone who can use, a "normie," gets involved with a person in recovery there is a tendency to think they are fine and to tempt them into using. "Come on honey, you can have just one, it's our anniversary." The choice to accept that temptation is theirs, but why shove temptation in their face? Would you really take someone addicted to gambling to a casino? If so,

that says more about you than them. This does not mean that being in a relationship with someone in recovery means you have to stop using. It is a delicate balance. You want to support the person in recovery and yet it's a choice and you need to be allowed to live your life. Early in recovery it can be helpful to not have alcohol or whatever substance they are addicted to in the home. This assumes they are working on the Big 8 and their brain is repairing itself.

4. **People do relapse.** The idea here is not to be paranoid about relapse. Doing so may heighten the pressure to use on the person in recovery. Remember, their behaviors are not going to change overnight and some may last a long time— behaviors associated with addiction. Asking them constantly if they are using is destructive. Trust has to be built up in all relationships. Trust them to tell you when they are having cravings or have relapsed without fear of judgment. It works both ways. They have to trust you and invite concerns. Relapse has to do with boundaries. We do not expect people to stay in relationships where someone relapses over and over again with no change in behavior to stop the cycle. What do you see different in the person's life?

5. **Recovery is a life-long process.** There is no cure. This means the person in recovery needs to be attentive to the disease. Recovery is not a cookie cutter; there is no one size fits all solution. We

know that regular attendance at AA (or something like it) and doing the "program" is the most successful method to date in recovery. The key question is, "Is it working?" Some people become fixated on AA or other forms of recovery. If the choice is AA or using, which do you want? The first year is the most critical. This does not mean they can stop doing what got them through their first year, but the hope is their brains will be repaired enough to allow for deep relationships and the time and commitment they take. Do not get into a relationship with a person in recovery if you are not committed to their sobriety. Are you willing to support them in going to meetings or other things that sustain and maintain recovery?

6. **Like often attracts like**. People in recovery tend to have many friends who are also in recovery. It makes sense. They must let go of those they used with or they will relapse. Hopefully some of those new friends will find a home in your relationship with the person in recovery as well. Everyone is wired differently. Some will have their lives dominated by people in recovery; others will not. What works? Having two completely separate and distinct lives does not work well in relationships for those in recovery. Are you able to attend a meeting now and then with the one in recovery? Do you attend Al-a-non?

7. **Working on the baggage**. Baggage is part of the addict's life. Avoiding it comes with a cost. They

need to face head-on their trauma, abuse, losses, and unmet needs. They need to work on their shame and guilt, repairing fractured relationships and other issues caused by their addiction. This is one of the steps in the 12-step program. They do an inventory of life, share that with others and repair what can be repaired. Can you support and encourage them through this process? Are you working on your own baggage? Think of it as literal baggage. You are at the baggage claim after a very long, hard trip. You have to get your two heavy pieces of luggage to the other end of the parking garage. How long will it take and how much pain will you endure if you do it alone? Get a cart? Have others with you to help?

8. **Recovery is self-discovery.** Depending on when a person became addicted and how long their brain has been hijacked, they may not know who they really are. Many addicts will say, "All I know is the addict." If addiction starts in the teens, their brains are not fully developed and they may have behaviors that are very adolescent, even if they are in their 50s. Addiction squashes maturity. This is another reason to give recovery time. The person at the start of recovery will be different than the one in recovery after a year. If you choose to enter into a deep relationship with someone early in recovery you need to be ready for this. We can always encourage self-growth. We do that best by growing ourselves.

9. **Accept them for who they are**. In all relationships we usually fail if we enter them thinking, *I can change them.* We accept people for who they are. If you are entering a relationship with an addict you need to understand that and accept it—that reality is not going to change. Addicts are amazing people and can handle relationships if fully engaged in ongoing recovery. People change at deep levels because they want to change, not because someone else wants them to change. They may adapt or be good at faking it, but in addiction we are after deep change. What does each of you bring to the relationship: the good, the bad, and the ugly?

10. **You have needs**. You may get into a relationship because you need to take care of someone. Where do feelings of worthiness, purpose, and fulfillment come? The true source of those needs to be internal. Yes, we need others in our lives. But being dependent on what any given person says or does in relation to you is Co-dependence and is unhealthy for you and the one in recovery.

11. Sometimes the Co-dependent person's issues are reflective of the addict's--two peas in a pod. If you put their needs consistently ahead of yours, you will both pay the price. This gets back to boundaries. Do a needs assessment, as you may have had the person in recovery do (see unmet needs section). What needs do you need to address? We all have them.

6. PURPOSE

We find that addiction and mental illness wreak havoc on purpose. We either lose our sense of purpose or we fail to live out the purposes we know we have. Both of those lead to anxiety, feelings of not being worthy, and a deepening of addiction and the symptoms of mental illness. It's a vicious cycle.

Sometimes purpose finds us. Most people who have a child feel it's their purpose to be a good parent. Most of the time we create our purpose in life; it doesn't come knocking at our door.

Purpose gives our life meaning, meaning and the fulfillment of purpose breed hope, hope creates resiliency and the desire to move forward. Purpose builds self-respect and self-esteem, counters shame and guilt and is a foundation of relationships.

Let's look at three levels of purpose: Try to list purposes you have in each category. If you don't have any, don't worry; just be honest.

As we work with those with chemical dependency issues, have conversations about their purposes in life. It is not your job to find them a purpose or to do whatever it takes to help them fulfill their purpose. Purpose is different than tasks. We do tasks in order to fulfill purpose. People go to meetings to stay sober and hopefully there is an underlying reason to stay sober. People who do not have a reason (internally) to stay sober usually fail. The reason, as

121

we have discussed, is that they need to be motivated by their own drive, not that of others. When addicts get clean solely because someone else wants them to, they relapse. Do they understand how important purpose is? Can they see how their addiction has taken a toll on their purposes in life? Do they understand that if they relapse they can't fulfill the purposes they have?

Knowing your purpose and working on the fulfillment of it can be of help to those in recovery. When talking with them, the following may be a short and useful tool. Remember, we are about hope, not shame. If they are struggling with finding purpose, it's ok; let's help them find some. Whenever we set goals for our lives we suggest using the SMARTS acronym, as discussed in a different chapter. It brings focus and accountability into the picture.

Addiction has only one purpose, the next fix of whatever the addiction is. Chemical dependency and all other addictions may allow for the semi-fulfillment of other purposes if the dependency is taken care of. It understands that in order to be fed it has to feed. That goes back to the reward system and to "compromise," if you see short periods of not giving into the addiction as compromise.

Short Term—what is your purpose over the next two weeks? Why are you/they here? Their purpose may simply be to stay clean and sober--a fantastic purpose. If they can't do that they will never find and fulfill their purpose. Work, housing, health, or a relationship may all be purposes in their lives over the next few weeks.

Internal—this is your/their purpose for you/them, such as getting sober or stable. The person in recovery has addiction in their brain; it is still running the show. What are they doing inside to change their thinking? What issues do they need to confront and how are they going to do that? If they are merely doing it on their own they will lose. They need a therapist, pastor, sponsor or friend who knows what they are doing. If they are on medications they will need to have one of their purposes being to take medications--all the time.

External—do you/they have a purpose relative to those around you/them? Do they have people they are responsible for or to? What are they doing about it? We do not want them to be overwhelmed with activity or guilt, but motivated to do something in these areas that they can be successful at, that will bring meaning to their lives, and keep them occupied. Isolation and inactivity are more often than not a significant reason for relapse.

Mid-Range—these are purposes they have over the next two weeks to nine months. Staying sober and doing the Big 8 should certainly be on the list. But there are undoubtedly others.

Internal—what are they meant to be doing over the next nine months for themselves? Why do they get up in the morning? What gets them excited or motivated? Part of purpose focuses on attending to the issues that brought on the addiction. Are they dealing with the trauma, abuse, or losses in their life? Are they diligently seeking to find and fill unmet needs? One of all our purposes should be to fill unmet needs. In so doing we bring our bodies, minds, and souls into a stronger place to be of help to others.

External—what are you meant to be doing for others and in the world over the next nine months? The internal and external purposes often overlap. When we act in ways that fulfill our external purposes we make inroads to our internal ones as well. When we do something that that helps our children, we also fulfill that internal sense of what it means to be a caring parent. This period of recovery is the most important neurobiologically. It is when the addiction is going to fight hardest to have the person relapse. Finding things to occupy time and give meaning to life is critical at this stage for long term recovery.

Long Range—these are purposes that you will have for a long time. Parenting might be one, perhaps a job, or a spiritual connection.

Internal--- Who are you meant to consistently be as a person; what values drive your purposes? What is their long term vision for themselves? Short- and mid-range purposes usually feed into the long term, but not always.

External-- How are they meant to give themselves to the world? What do they offer? At times this is where shame shows up, for they feel they have nothing to offer. That is chemical dependency speaking. We can help them find the value they can't find within themselves.

If they have blanks, it's a great place to look at their support network and see how they might be able to help find purpose. What talents and interests do they have? How can they use those to better themselves and the world around them? Do their purposes build self-esteem and create positive and meaningful relationships?

Do they believe they can find and fulfill purpose in their life? If they continue to use substances or remain unstable will those purposes be fulfilled? Probably not. Creating and fulfilling purpose pleases our brains. Finding purpose will help their depression, anxiety, and addiction.

We can help by making their purposes clear to them, supporting them as they seek to fill them, and giving them a kick when they get off track. Remember, it is not your job to find and fill their purposes. If they are not invested in their recovery, they will not recover.

7.   **Unmet Needs**-- See section on unmet needs—we all have them and when some needs are unmet it has a significant negative impact on our lives and minds.

Just a note on an unmet need we have not focused on but that can be very important in recovery: MEDICATIONS-- Addiction changes and hijacks the brain. Most people vastly underestimate the power of addiction on the brain. There are times when medications can significantly help with cravings. The goal is not to be on medications for addiction for life, but to gradually get off them as the ability to cope and the degree to which the Big 8 are being enacted take place. No one on any kind of medication should ever just stop. Always do it under a doctor's supervision. In addiction, sudden withdrawal from medications significantly increases chances for relapse.

Chemical dependency often goes hand in hand with other issues such as depression, anxiety, or other mental illness diagnoses. Medications can help those as well. Doctors should be consulted about the various combinations of medications.

8. Spirituality-- For those for whom spirituality is or has been an important part of their lives, this can be an incredible and underrated asset. There is no right or wrong way to do spirituality; it's ensuring we connect with that which is greater than us. Because everyone has their own spirituality we will not go in depth on the subject here. The following are four areas of spirituality that need to be attended to for those who take their spirituality seriously.

Fellowship (getting together with others who are on a similar spiritual journey)—As John Dunne said, "No man is an island unto himself." Our brains are wired for connection and fellowship is an important part of that. Twelve-step programs are great places for fellowship for those in recovery. Depending on what your spirituality is based on that may not be the only fellowship they are a part of. Far too many people believe fellowship is not that important. There is not a spirituality on earth that believes that. Yes there are times when being alone is called for, but community solidifies the journey, gives us a place to be held accountable, and gives us a feedback loop for when our thoughts go astray-- which everyone's does.

Study (learning about the spirituality we profess to be a part of)—Whether it is reading the Big Book, the Bible, Quran, Buddha's sermons or a wide list of other sacred writings, we all need to study those who have gone before us and share their wisdom. Why reinvent the wheel? We encourage people to learn from all faiths even though they relate to one. Buddhists can learn from Christians and vice versa. The key is to find what works, what keeps us stable and clean, gives us strength, feeds our purpose, fills our needs, and helps us feel we are worthy.

Prayer/Meditation (connecting directly with that which is beyond)—There are many ways to pray and meditate; the key is finding out which one strengthens the one in recovery, helps them to hear the voice of sobriety instead of addiction and helps them to reach out to others when they are in need. Meditating or praying with no change in behaviors or how we think and feel is useless. If what you/they are doing doesn't work, try a different style. Discipline in all of these areas is critical. Doing any of these now and then will not strengthen the spirit. What can you/they do consistently that you can commit to? Prayer and meditation--all aspects of spirituality--are very helpful to people in and out of recovery. Those helping those in recovery need strength as well. Where is that strength coming from?

Service (reaching out to others because we are driven to do it by our spiritual practice). Addiction is a self-centered disease. What is the person doing to get out of him- or herself and start living for others? Going to meetings is great and serving there is a wonderful thing to do but it is still focused on them. True service has very little to do with self and more to do with getting out of self for others. What do they enjoy doing? They could volunteer at an animal shelter, church, school, soup kitchen, or a wide variety of other options. Remember that connection with others, purpose, and fun are all part of what needs to be paid attention to. Many forms of service can fill all those at the same time. Like most other things, most addicts do not do a lot of service while using.

Spirituality is about something that is bigger than us. In addiction it is about those things that we believe can help us in recovery because we know we can't do it alone. Many people on their first attempt to control their use believe they can do it alone. Some take multiple attempts before they acknowledge they need support, encouragement, and help. Spirituality is about admitting this truth and living it out in our lives. Spirituality in part is about getting out of ourselves in order to be there for others. We understand that we do not truly find ourselves until we connect and live with and for others. Paying attention only to others and sacrificing ourselves is not healthy either; life seeks balance.

Below is a list of questions around spiritual themes. They were written for use by those in recovery, but you can change the wording to work for your situation if need be.

Purpose:
-List as many purposes as you can think of that you have currently in your life and how they can be viewed from a

spiritual angle. You can think of purposes in the following way if it's helpful:

Short term—Purposes you have that will be done in less than two months (for example—get sober, find housing, find a job)

Mid-range—two months to nine months (get into school, get and keep a job, start to heal relationship with family member)

Long-range – nine months – rest of life—(being a parent, writing, being involved with service work)

-Do you believe that addiction has impacted purposes in your life?

-On a scale of 1-10, 10 being a life filled with purpose, where would you put yourself?

-Where do the purposes above come from? You, family, others, culture, religious ideas (God).

-If you believe in a divine presence, can you identify a specific "calling" or purpose it has given you? How is that purpose "spiritual?"

-What do you think you can do in the next month to find purpose or to more fully fulfill your purposes? Use the SMART goal setting form to come up with a plan.

Meaning:

-What gives meaning to your life?

-On a scale of 1-10, 10 being lots of meaning, how meaningful is your life?

-What do you think would make your life more meaningful?

-Who are three people you admire (living or dead)? What do you think brought meaning to their lives?

-How has your addiction affected meaning in your life?
-If you believe in a divine presence, how does that presence help you with making sense of your life and the issues within it?

Relationships:
-What are the most meaningful relationships in your life? List them. Why are they meaningful?
-When you think about those relationships, how much of the focus is on you? On them?
-Have your relationships have been affected by addiction? How? How would you describe relationships you have with other people with chemical dependency issues and those with people who do not have those issues?
-What kind of a relationship would be most useful for you to create at this time in your life? If it is with someone you know, how can you start to make that happen? If it's with someone you don't know, where will you find that person or persons?
-If you believe in a divine presence, how would you describe your relationship with it? Is that what you want it to look like? What can you do to change the relationship? What has that relationship done for you and to you in the past?
-Are there things in you, other than addiction, getting in the way of building relationships?

Creativity:
-You are a creative person; how do you use your creativity? Don't think of being creative as only something artistic, but as how you approach something. You can be a creative counselor, teacher, custodian, athlete, etc.

-If you don't see yourself as creative, why is that? Where did that idea come from?
-Has addiction affected your creativity? How?
-Where does your creativity come from? Yourself? Others? Culture? God?
-If you believe in a divine presence, what "gifts" has that presence given you to be creative with? If you don't believe that you have been given gifts, why not?
-What can you do to use your creativity more? What, other than addiction, is getting in the way?

Self-Image:
-How would you describe yourself? You might make a list of five or ten words or phrases you would use (good, bad, or ugly). How do you think others see you? (Ask others to give you five words they would use to describe you and see how they compare to your words.
-How has your "using" affected your view of yourself?
-What part of your self-image is most destructive? Why?
-What part of how you see yourself would you most like to change? How can you do that? Use the SMARTS goal strategy to come up with a plan.
-Do you have others in your life that believe in you, lift you up, support you? (This includes spiritual beings.)
-If you believe in a divine presence, how do you think that presence would describe you? What is different from your own way of seeing yourself and why?
-What are three things you can do to improve your self-image? This may include being more honest with yourself if you have a better self-image than perhaps you should have.

THE BIG 8

So we have looked at Sleep, Exercise, Nutrition, Fun, Connection, Purpose, Unmet needs, and Spirituality. If they wake up each day and ask themselves what they can do in each of those areas to better their life, if they go to bed at night and look at this list and can tell themselves (honestly) they've done something in each area, their life will change. Those who relapse look at the list and find several, if not all of these areas have become deficient in their lives as they slide into relapse.

Addiction likes to put things into drawers, or at least out of sight. This list needs to be on the fridge, bathroom mirror and/or front door—in plain sight.

MYTHS AND TRUTHS

Below, in no certain order, is a list of common myths about addiction, along with some added truths.

1. Myth—**Just Stop!!-- Addicts can just stop if they want to**— You know from reading this book that this is not true. Addiction literally changes the wiring in the brain. This myth believes you can instantly become a concert pianist. The myth lacks understanding of the neurobiology of addiction. Most chemically dependent people have a great deal of will power, but that internal power has been focused on using. In recovery, addiction does not give up easily. It takes effort and time to shift

one's will power from using to sobriety. Part of addiction is located in an area of the brain called the mesolimbic dopamine system that is not under conscious control. The changes in the brain enhance the dependencies' ability to create internal and external situations where using makes imminent sense to the user. Cravings increase, impulse control decreases, and compulsions to use increase. This is especially true in the first six months. This is not an excuse for them to use, but those helping addicts need to be very aware of what they are dealing with and how difficult recovery can be.

2. Myth-- **Addicts can't be productive**-- All of us know addicts that are productive, even in active addiction. We probably all know people who are addicted that we would be surprised about. Percentage-wise, very few are the stereotypical alcoholic. High functioning addicts are the norm. Addiction does take a toll on all aspects of life. In helping someone in recovery we need to be very careful not to judge them. They may have made some serious errors in life but we do not help by judging. We help by trying to assist them in becoming more productive--purpose, service. When the human brain is given the chance to repair, it is stunning what changes take place.

3. Myth--**Addiction is picky about who it chooses,** usually those with low standards, low income, and minimum education. Chemical dependency does

not discriminate. It treats everyone equally. We have discussed how there is a genetic component and how underlying much of addiction are issues of trauma, abuse, and/or significant loss. None of these have a bias either. Addiction is found within all educational and socioeconomic levels. While there are age groupings that tend to have a higher rate of addiction onset, dependency is not concerned with age. Religion, culture, and ethnicity are also not good indicators. Yes, there are ethnicities that are more prone to addiction, but there is no ethnicity that is exempt. Addicts often have very high ethical and moral standards and a strong value system, all of which do poorly with active users. Internally the person knows they are living up to their own value system so they feel guilty--another reason to use.

4. Myth--**The disease concept means the addict has a disease--there is nothing you can do about it--** There is no cure; we talked about that earlier when we discussed the brain and the receptors. Addiction is a unique disease. We can't take a picture of it until very late in a chronic addict's life. For most addicts the damage and rewiring of the brain can be changed. So yes, it is a disease and there is no cure, but there is permanent, enduring remission. The addict may state it is too late for them. There is never a "too late." None of us knows what the brain is capable of unless we give it a chance.

5. Myth—**We should excuse bad behaviors due to addiction** -- We all make choices in life, some good ones and some that are not so good. We should all be responsible for choices we make—especially as adults. We live in an entitlement culture which consistently excuses bad behaviors. This is not helpful to the addict. Actions have consequences. This gets back to boundaries. We help people in recovery by having clear boundaries and by living up to them. The chemically dependent person may not be completely responsible for their disease, but they are for their recovery and their actions. Addicts are not bad people; they are sick people trying to get well.

6. Myth--**Relapse is part of addiction and repeated relapse means there is no hope—** We are talking about a disease. People with diseases often have "relapses." Diabetics have periods of instability in their blood sugar. People with cholesterol issues have their ups and downs. All diseases come with a struggle, one that demands energy, attention, and diligence. Addiction is a chronic and progressive disease if not checked. Relapse is not failure; it's relapse. Helping the addict to see that and being careful not to judge the relapse can go a long way. Again, this does not excuse the use and there may be consequences for that relapse, but we are focusing on the behavior, not the person.

7. Myth--**Alcohol and drug use cause addiction--** There is no chemical dependency if a person does

not use and there are many more people who use and do not become addicted than do. We do not have a full understanding about why and when a person moves from use to abuse to dependency. We have talked about this in more detail in a different chapter. While it may be useful to understand the origins of a person's addiction, it is not critical to recovery unless that issue is still active in someone's life. A person who experienced severe trauma and uses to avoid the impact of that trauma on their lives has a high chance of relapse. They decrease that chance by facing and dealing with the trauma.

8. Myth—**It's better to punish addicts with severe consequences than to treat them**-- Addiction is a disease of choice, a very seductive one that starts off innocently and then imprisons a person's brain. Do we punish those with diabetes, hypertension, or autism? There should always be consequences for inappropriate actions, no matter what the situation. Those consequences depend on what took place and with whom; there is no black and white. But are the consequences seen as the end or is there a positive treatment alternative in addition to the consequences? Addiction is a treatable disease if those with it admit they have the disease and are willing to do something about it. We need to do our best to separate actions done by a person from the person doing the actions. Inside everyone is something good wanting to be set free.

9. Myth—**Those who are dependent on one thing are ultimately dependent on all things**-- Addiction rewires the brain and many people become cross-addicted. They convince themselves that if they give up alcohol they can handle pills. The majority of the time this is not true. Remember, we are talking about the receptors in the brain and there are a lot of them and a lot of different kinds. There are those with addictive personalities. That should be dealt with, but if someone needs to be addicted to something, why not exercise, reading, or serving others?

10. Myth--**Medications can't fix addictions**-- This is currently true. A hundred years of research and hundreds of millions of dollars have not found a medicinal "fix" for addiction. Medications can be very, very helpful in recovery. We discussed this in an earlier chapter. Some medications to help with cravings are not addictive; others can be. Conversations with a doctor who understands addiction are important in dealing with medications. Antabuse, Naltrexone, Vivitrol, Subutex, Suboxone, Methadone, and Acomprasate are the main ones used at this time. During withdrawal (detox) some of these and others are used to ease the physical symptoms. The idea of medications is to help the brain be in a place where it can do the work needed to sustain recovery. If the things we have been talking about that lead to addiction and relapse are not faced and dealt with, medications will not fix the brain.

11. Myth—**Just go to AA; that is all you need to do**-- We are profound believers in AA; it is the best tool available for sustained recovery. If you look at what AA does, it deals with all the aspects of the brain we have discussed and many of the Big 8. AA does not work for everyone and some people become "addicted" to AA (which is far better than using). As is true with all things in life, a balance should be sought and that is different for everyone. AA can bring support, understanding, non-judgment, accountability, a safe haven and harbor, proximity (see section on attachment), fun, connections, purpose, spirituality, and can certainly fill some unmet needs. It is not a solution for all issues in one's life.

12. Myth—**"My doctor prescribed the medication; it must be safe"** – We live in a world of over-prescribed medications. A doctor should know of addictive issues in your life before prescribing anything. Pain medications are currently vastly abused and easily lead to addiction. As dosages go up and length of use goes on, questions should be raised before addiction sets in.

13. Myth--**"Natural" medications are safer and better than those made in a lab**-- Some people will say that marijuana and other substances are OK because they are natural. They still alter brain chemistry and can produce side effects and addiction. Before using any of them, consult a

138

doctor—and yes, medical marijuana cards are over-prescribed as well.

14. Myth—**High tolerance means there is no problem**—Some people will say they drink a lot with no issue. Ask them if that was true the first time they started drinking. Using a lot and that amount having no or little impact means their brain has adapted to that amount. This is not a good sign and means they need help sooner rather than later. Some alcoholics are highly functional—for a time. The disease of addiction always catches up. We do not understand the mechanism of "high functioning" addiction fully. If a person is addicted there will always be changes in behaviors. Sometimes we are around the person falling into addiction. The changes are slow and we don't notice them; we adapt our own behaviors and thoughts in relation to their changes. This is what enabling is at times.

15. Myth—**Drug addiction is a choice**-- USE is a choice. Using over an extended period of time changes the brain and becomes abuse and then addiction. Addiction is not a choice.

16. Myth—**Once detoxed, addiction is asleep**—Most people will state they feel great and are "good to go" after detox. Their brains do not rewire for months at best. The addictive brain is highly active and motivated early in recovery. Most relapses happen in the first six months of recovery and one

of the main reasons people relapse between six months and a year is because of overconfidence; "I've been sober a year, I can handle one." There is no cure, period. Recovery is a life-long process.

17. Myth—**If someone uses again, they instantly return to how life was before recovery**-- We know that biologically most addicts will return to the amount of usage before they stopped very quickly. Many people slip, realize their mistake and stop before the destruction starts again. Relapse in and of itself can become a pattern. We want people to have as few relapses (if any) as possible. It's about motivation. What is the reason to stay clean? How will they be rewarded if they do?

18. Myth--**You have to be spiritual to get and stay sober**-- The idea is to understand that there is something greater than the addiction. If the addict is all there is and they believe they can do it all on their own, they will lose. The "other" does not need to be spiritual. Smart Recovery is one method people use without spirituality. We do know that for those with spirituality it can be an immense asset and addiction does its best to undermine that spirituality because of its power. AA believes in spirituality but does not specify what spirituality that is.

19. Myth—**Alcoholism is better than drug addiction—** If you take this literally, the truth is far from it. Alcoholism causes significantly more damage to the

economy, relationships, and health issues than other drugs. All addiction is destructive; we should not say one is better or worse than the other. They are all diseases.

20. Myth—**Addicts have to hit rock bottom before they change**—Everyone has a bottom where change takes place and everyone's bottom is different. For one, their first DUI might be enough. For another the loss of job, family, and friends may be their bottom. There are those who will die before hitting bottom. The hope is that we can raise the bottom. How can we help someone see what they are losing because of their addiction? Interventions are based on the idea of collectively raising the awareness of the addict of how their using is negative impacting their lives and the lives of those around them. This raises the bottom. The bottom exists when an addict says, "Enough is enough."

In addition to all of these it's important to understand that you have rights. You have the right to say, "I'm done." Addiction has the right to say, "I'm going to use." Rights only exist if we use them. Sometimes we make a choice to allow someone to walk on our rights—our choice and yes, some choices are very, very difficult. The choice to use may include losing a relationship, job, health, or life. The choice to leave a relationship where an addict refuses to stop may be a significant loss that requires grieving. There may be a financial price to pay--it's still a choice. We all need to own our choices. It's a good exercise to see what rights you believe you have. Is there anything you believe you do not have the right to—especially with an addict or one in recovery? Where does that come from? Have you asked others what they think about how you think?

CHAOS THEORY AS A METAPHOR IN RECOVERY

Chaos theory has become part of our cultural language. Founded through discoveries in weather patterns and mathematical equations, its insights are far-reaching. This chapter will not delve into the scientific reality of chaos theory but will focus on a few key ideas that are part of the theory and how they apply to addiction, mental illness, and recovery in both.

Everyone agrees that active addiction and mental illness lead to chaos, internally and in the lives of those involved. We buy a deck of cards and they are all ordered. Throw them in the air and chaos reigns. It takes energy and focus to bring the deck back into order. What is interesting about any game of cards is that they always start in chaos; the deck is never ordered. The challenge is how well does each player deal with chance?

While no human's life is "ordered," when we add addiction and/or mental illness, the levels of chaos are significantly increased. We talk in life about being "normal." Technically normal is what is average; there is no normal unless we give authority to someone to determine what normal is. Our lives are littered with the ebbs and flows of stress. For whatever reason, we have all developed different coping skills to deal with those stressors in our lives. Like addiction, they become habitual.

Part of the process in recovery is learning new coping skill habits.

Addiction is at its essence chaotic, yet we find order within the chaos. We have come to very clear understandings about how addiction impacts the brain and hijacks it. We have come to some very good ideas about how it all starts and what it takes to get control of the brain back. What follows is not about understanding chaos or learning to live it, it's about using what we know about chaotic systems to help those who live with the addict and the addict themselves to thrive in recovery and protect themselves from relapse.

The principles of chaos theory give us a deeper understanding of how this all gets started and what we can do to change those patterns and help others as well.

BUTTERFLY EFFECT

Many have heard of the idea of the butterfly effect. A butterfly flaps its wings somewhere, changes ever so slightly the air current around it, which because of everything else winds up being a hurricane. While this may be a bit drastic, the bottom line is that hurricanes do start somewhere and the initial conditions of the hurricane matter.

Think of a forest fire. There is a reason there are no significant forest fires during winter or the rainy season: the initial conditions are not there. In the summer, when there has been a drought for five years and there is a great deal of dry grass or underbrush, fires are more likely to start and expand.

Addiction started somewhere in each addict's life. Playing the blame game does not work. Addicts need to accept the responsibility that they chose to use, regardless of the underlying issues in their lives. We can't go back and change the past, we can only move forward to a different future. We have already looked at how genetics, trauma, abuse, grieving, and unmet needs were probably some of the initial conditions that got the disease moving. When a person begins the recovery process, a new set of initial conditions begins.

One of the challenges for those living or working with the addicted is to find out how we can best help support those conditions. The addict has to do the work, but those who do it alone fail. Those helping in recovery at times feel helpless. They are confronted with a disease they don't understand and are at a loss as what to do. It seems so simple--just stop!! It is an ongoing discussion as to whether or not those who are able to "just stop" were ever truly addicted in the first place.

So what can someone do to best aid a person in recovery that helps with initial conditions?

1. **Learn about addiction**. Simply by reading this book you are hopefully learning at deeper level things you had not known or understood before. This means learning about the myths and realities of addiction and living out the reality rather than buying into the myth. We all know that actions speak much louder than words and this is true both for the addicted and those living with or helping them. Understanding addiction can take us from being judgmental and blaming to being more supportive and less enabling.

2. **Be clear.** It is very important for addicts to know where they stand. Setting clear expectations, hopes, and boundaries is very important. Make sure you are able and willing to stand by what you say. For example, if you say, "If you drink, you are no longer living in this house or you are fired, or I will not be communicating with you," and they use and you say, "Ok, next time I mean it," you have already told them you don't mean it, that your "line in the sand" is meaningless. Count the cost of accountability before you dive in.

3. **Ask.** Ask the addicted how you can be most helpful and supportive. Ultimately, they are in the driver's seat. They feel immense pressure and that adds to the stress they already have. Remember, their brain has been rewired; it does not change overnight. This is not an excuse for relapse or bad behavior; it helps them understand how precarious recovery is. Let them know you are truly listening to them. Repeat back to them what you are hearing, show them by what you do that you have heard. Perhaps put a list up on the refrigerator of what you can do to help if you live with them.

Asking the addicted about their addiction can be very educational--when they are not using. They see things differently than those who are not addicted. Getting them to open up about their ups and downs, their struggles and fears, and their successes is an important step for them and for you.

You can also ask others who have been on this journey for a while. Going to Al-a-non meetings can be helpful. While each addiction has its own characteristics, there are a lot of common themes throughout addiction. You can go to an Al-a-non meeting and learn tools that will help you as you deal with someone addicted to gambling or other things.

There is a balance between showing concern and being annoying. Addicts are very sensitive to this. Asking someone every 20 minutes how they are doing is annoying. Checking in is helpful. What addicts need to know is that you are there for them, in a non-judgmental, non-critical way. Asking questions is better than making statements: How were cravings today? What did you do for recovery today? Any big stressors in your life today? Anything I can do to help today?

4. **Create a positive environment**-- Addicts are in for the struggle of their lives. Their brain has been wired for addiction and it is not giving up easily. Creating an environment where they are supported, not judged, with clear boundaries, open communication, and accountability, is important. The degree to which the environment you are a part of can aid in that will be beneficial to them. Be affirming. Remember that the reward system (rewarding them for using) helped get their brains in trouble. All of us respond more positively when we are rewarded for our behaviors, internally and externally. This is not to suggest you have a "prize" out there for not giving into the addiction. But

celebrating is very important. What that looks like for you and for them is ultimately up to you, but rewards work.

It is not that helpful initially in the early stages of recovery to look at the initial conditions of the addiction itself. Certainly those conditions led to the addiction taking over. This is not looking for excuses--there are none--but rather seeking understanding to work through issues or guard against relapses. Therapy, journal writing, and AA can all be useful resources toward this end. The focus in early recovery is getting that six months of sobriety. Looking to the past can be a distraction and a trigger.

STRANGE ATTRACTORS

The idea of a black hole is a good metaphor for strange attractors. Our brains are wired from birth for certain things. You can call it instinct, survival mode, the need to be loved, the need to act ethically, or whatever you'd like to call it. These things are attractors; they act as gravitational fields in our minds and bodies. We can view a genetic predisposition to addiction as a strange attractor. It is something within addicts that pulls them to addiction. This does not mean they have to go to that attraction, but it is there. Below is a diagram of a double strange attraction-- an addicted brain and a brain in recovery— both are literally fighting for control of the individual. Both are at war to control the different parts of the brain we have discussed earlier. In addiction, when we give power and authority to one of the attractors, the other diminishes. As with the Butterfly Effect, we want to create the best initial conditions possible to give the strange attractor of the sober and stable brain the best chance to grow.

Recovery is about circling these attractors, each with their own "pull." Cravings are a way the addicted brain seeks to pull those in recovery back. The challenge for those helping those in recovery is to understand the psychological and physiological pull of addiction, that it is one of these strange attractors. The unaddicted have a very hard time understanding this pull; it's not part of their universe. But it is very real, and calling the addicted "weak," "immoral," "bad," or other judgmental words is not helpful. Again, this is not to let them off the hook or give them an excuse (there are none), but it is to call us all to a deeper understanding of the power of the addiction— the strange attractor. Let's remember that addiction is doing something for them—along with all the destruction. A question for those without addiction is "what is your strange attractor?" We all have them. What has significant "gravity" in your life? Can the addict see how their addiction has become a strange attractor in their life?

Strange attractors are wired into our brains through habits and culture. The more we iterate (go through the cycle), the more powerful the attractor itself becomes. Note that in the diagram the attractor is always being circled: the line comes close to being consumed and then swings out. This is true in addiction until the end, when a person succumbs to it and dies. Something in their lives needs to give them more than the addiction does. If you change a value within the equation that creates this graph by just a little, you will see significant changes taking place as the attractor shifts. That is what we want in addiction, to shift the center of the attractor.

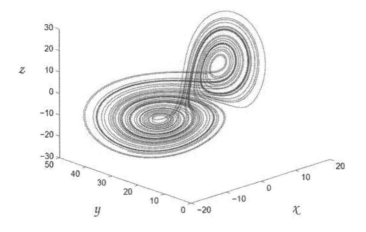

https://www.skepticalscience.com/print.php?r=134

How to help create strong positive strange attractors:
1. The Big 8 are all attractors in their own way. Our bodies need those things to function well. Unless something upsets the natural rhythm of life, we have a tendency to do those things.
2. Help the person to see that these "gravitational forces" exist in their lives and they don't simply go away without diligence and effort. Denial is denying these exist in their lives.
3. One can also look at the different parts of our lives and see how attractors are at work there. Look at family, social interactions, work, the physical body, spiritual presence, mental state of being, intuition, and emotions. In systems we tend to conform

more than we like to admit. There is nothing wrong with conforming as long as the attractor is positive and healthy. Where are other negative or positive attractors found in life?

4. Gravity is created by mass—amounts. The more of the Big 8 a person creates in their life, the more gravity they have. The chemically dependent person is trying to create such gravity in their lives that it weighs down the addiction.

5. As is true with everything, talking about what is going on is important. How do they see the attractors working in their lives? Cravings and triggers are types of attractors; how are those going? Those who do not reach out when being pulled by a negative attractor do not do well. They need to find a positive attractor (often another person) and use their gravity to keep them going. The earth is in a fine balance with the sun. Part of the earth wants to fly off into space and yet is held in balance by the gravity of the sun. We all need to find and use the positive attractors in our lives.

BIFURCATION

"Two roads diverged in a wood and I - I took the one less traveled by, and that has made all the difference." Robert Frost

This famous quote from a wonderful poem by Robert Frost sums up the notion of bifurcation. In a purely ordered system, every time there is a fork in the road, the exact same (and correct) choice is made. But we all know this never happens. We think of computers as being "perfect." It's all math and electronics; what can go wrong? Yet things do.

When you realize that the human brain has 2,000,000,000,000 (trillion) connections, are we surprised that the wiring doesn't get messed up? We should be stunned that it doesn't go haywire more than it does. Every human being is faced with thousands of conscious decisions every day and probably millions of unconscious ones (like breathing, having a heartbeat, blinking, and walking). The brain is behind every one of those. A small percent of those decisions are consciously made, and when we make a decision we make a choice.

The addict has a choice to make every time they use. At some point the decision becomes easy, and then they have to make decisions about lying, manipulating, hurting others, cheating, stealing, hiding, and a myriad of other choices to maintain the addiction.

Every decision we make impacts all future decisions. The more decisions an addict makes to go with the addictive path in the brain, the deeper that rut becomes as the "norm." Here is a diagram of a mathematical bifurcation.

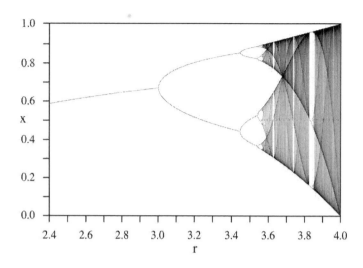

https://en.wikipedia.org/wiki/Bifurcation_diagram

As you can see, we diverge quickly from any given path. You couple this idea with the Butterfly Effect and it becomes easier to see how quickly things can go wrong— or right.

For the addicted there is a road sign at every juncture: Use and Don't Use, Do or Don't Do. To tell someone the choice is easy only shows ignorance and a severe lack of empathy. The choice for many is excruciatingly difficult, especially in the first six months. The process for the addict has been easy—say yes and do what it takes to make the yes work. When confronted with the reality of what making those choices is doing, the addict breaks through denial and has a desire to change. Choosing the road less travelled is far from easy. We are all creatures of habit; our tendency is to go the direction of least resistance, that which we know, that which is easiest—why would we expect anything different from the addicted?

Think of a habit you have taken on--a new language, a musical instrument, becoming a good artist or cook, a runner, etc. Our guess is that it didn't all come with ease; there were times you struggled and wondered if it was worth it. No one becomes a concert pianist without a great deal of effort, discipline, and sacrifice. The same is true in recovery and those starting recovery need to count the cost and understand what they are in for. The end result is worth it, but thinking that the addictive brain is going down without a fight is being naïve.

So how can we help those in recovery with this bifurcation process?

1. Have discussions about decisions they make, not in a judgmental way, but with empathy. What people, places, and things, will get in their way of recovery and what help do they need in order to make the right decision before they get to that fork in the road?
2. Many junctions in roads have signs pointing which direction to go. If you have no map or signs how would you know? Be a map or have a map ready. AA, books, therapists, Al-a-non are all good maps for the addicted and those helping them. There is no need to reinvent the wheel, just learn what works and help those do what needs to be done.
3. Understand that every decision is a potentially important one. The idea that an alcoholic can have "just one beer" is insanity. One leads to two leads

to four leads to disaster. It would be fantastic if that were true, but we know it isn't. Not all decisions are equal. The decision to have a Coke or a Pepsi is not equal to whether or not to have a baby, go to college, take a job, or use one's drug of choice. We all know which decisions in our lives are the important ones. We don't always know where a decision will lead, but we can be assured that for an addict, the choice to use will lead to destruction. The choice to stay in recovery opens options and opportunities. The choice to use closes options.

4. Share your own choices in life, the struggles you have. Empathy is about saying, "Me too." It's not about having the same exact struggles, but understanding the idea of struggle. Which would be more powerful for you to hear when you are struggling: "Come on, suck it up, don't be a wimp, just do it, don't let us down" or "I hear your struggle, I know you are in the battle of your life, but I believe in you, I believe you can do this and make the right choice as hard as that may be, and I'm here to help if you want." We hope it's number 2. Number 1 breeds shame and guilt, especially if they relapse, which they might.

SELF-ORGANIZATION

Many things in biological systems self-organize. Our DNA organizes after conception to create a human being. With the billions of new cells created, things go wrong. Our cellular state of being continues to self-organize in spite of these changes and mutations. The brain has shown itself to be highly plastic, to be able to adapt to a wide variety of physical and environmental changes. Global or system-wide patterns exist in spite of smaller patterns of individual components of the system. Addiction is a system that organizes itself around survival of the disease. We hear of "functional" addicts, people who use and seem to do quite well in life. This may be true for a period of time, but addiction always catches up with us. Because it is physically, mentally, emotionally, and socially having to adapt, it reorganizes constantly around new lies, manipulations, and secrecy. The adaptations themselves create a need to escape from the false sense of reality they are creating.

On a larger scale we see how birds flock, schools of fish swim and herds of animals gather, all for survival, warmth, ease of locomotion, communication, and protection. Human groups self-organize for many of the same reasons.

Our brains organize around principles that we set forth to the brain—once we have the ability to do so. In youth, choices are made for our brain, we are exposed to environments that are not of our own choosing and those environments play a significant role on how we adapt to and cope with the environments and the stress they cause that surround us. The brain organizes itself around addiction or sobriety. It does its best to maintain a world that can be viably addicted until the amount and depth of that addiction are so destructive the brain can no longer cope.

Here the hope is to reorganize before reaching that point. There are many components in the world of addiction. If you are part of the addict's life, then you are one of the components. How you act and react makes a difference in how the addict self-organizes. Those of us in the mental health professions that deal with addiction are some of those components. Medications we give or don't give, what we say, how we treat clients, how we respect them and yet speak the truth, and how we hear and respond to their story are all ways their self-organization is helped or hindered. Is our message one of hope or of doom, of support or of "you are on your own?" This becomes increasingly difficult the more a person relapses and the greater the damage done to the relationship. The addict loses hope that they can change and when the world around them agrees and gives them evidence that they are right, the end is probably not far off. Those of us with hope need to bring that hope to those who need it, and the need is vast. The addict needs to make the choice but success is much more likely if they know there is support in that struggle.

So how can we help someone in the throes of addiction to transform their self-organization in a new direction—to recovery?

1. Find out what the person believes about themselves. Self-image and self-organization go hand in hand. While doing that, what do you believe about yourself? What do you or they believe about the world around them? One way of doing this is asking them to write down five words they would use to describe themselves: good, bad, or ugly. See what they say. Has their addiction robbed them of those words? You can also go

online and find a list of values. Have them list or put a check mark by all the values that are very important in their lives. Then have them rate how they are living those values out as a user (1-10—1 being not well and 10 being perfectly). Most addicts have a lot of high values and a lot of low numbers when it comes to living them out. Our values flow from our self-image. When we do not live out the life we claim to value, we have to cope with that; denial, avoidance, defensiveness, fear, and addiction are all strategies.

2. Help them change their image by affirmations. This is not a call to lie. If someone relapses we don't congratulate them. We can make the statement: "I'm sorry you relapsed, I know what a difficult journey this is. I believe you want to stop and I believe you can stop. What can you do differently this time to avoid that same pitfall and is there something I can do to help?" Note that we do not judge or critique the person, just the behaviors.

3. Sit with the person who needs to self-organize and ask them this: "What are the components in your life that lead you to organize around addiction and what are the components that lead you to sobriety? Write them down." They should be able to come up with a list of people, places, and things in both categories. Push them to be specific. If they say "users", ask them what users.

Questions can be dangerous. There are times when the person asking the question might be part of the problem. For example, you might be in denial yourself. You are trying to help them, but your own addiction or other issues are a component of their addiction. The person responding needs to feel they can be vulnerable and speak the truth or they will maintain the status quo.

4. Somehow in all self-organizing structures, be it a crystal, school of fish, flock of geese, or human brain, each component needs to understand its connection to the others. The addict is part of a system. When the system is perceived as being against them, there is little energy to change and lots of evidence to not change. Addicts need to be aware of their disease's impact on the system; that is what interventions are about--people sharing specific examples about how the addiction has damaged their lives and the life of the system--be it family, friends, work, or other.

FRACTALS

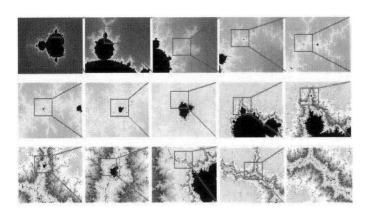

http://www.meta-synthesis.com/webbook/24_complexity/complexity.html

We have heard a lot about fractals in the past 30 years. We see them everywhere in nature and in mathematics. The above diagram is called the Mandlebrot Set. It is an equation where you take a set of numbers, put them into the equation and when you get an answer, you put that back into the equation. You do that thousands of times and you graph the results. What we find is pretty remarkable. When you zoom in on any part of the diagram, as seen above, you see repeating patterns. You can zoom in 10,000-fold and you will still see the same pattern. We see this in addiction.

We understand very well the biological, neurological, mental, emotional, social, and spiritual patterns of addiction. While every individual has specific ways it manifests in their lives, the patterns are the same: lying, hiding, cheating, manipulating, and denying. There are consistent and persistent stages of addiction that we recognize. These patterns over time not only exist in relation to the addiction but overflow to other areas of life. Being in denial about addiction leads to denial of other issues in life. We all know that lying breeds lying. When an addict enters recovery they are not simply stopping using or stopping a behavior, they are having to change how their entire being has adapted to that disease. None of us goes from A to Z overnight.

Think of a very dense jungle that you cannot walk through without a machete or bulldozer. You hack a path through it and you use that path over and over again until it is clear. That is what addiction is, a clear and "easy" path. When an addict enters recovery they put a gate at the entrance to the path and are handed a machete to make a new path. If you have a choice to take the easy path you know or forge a new one that takes immense amounts of effort and sweat, which would you take? We should not be shocked at relapse. We are more likely to cut a new path if we know we are not alone, that while we will be doing most of the work, there are others there to support and encourage us. What happens when a new path is cut to the old path? It grows over. The longer the old path is not used the harder it is to uncover and the more the new path is used the easier it becomes to stay on that path. The ideas in this book are about making that new path.

When we look at an addict's life, we look for patterns that are destructive to the system, patterns in all areas of life. One aspect of addiction is how the addict pulls the non-addict into their system. Many of us are in denial about someone's addiction. Partly because our culture still sees it as weakness rather than as a disease, we don't want to see someone that way. It's easier to turn our heads and minds to denial. When we are in denial we become enablers.

The process of taking an answer to an equation and putting it back into the equation is called an iteration. Addiction does the same thing. In the beginning an alcoholc drinks and feels good. Slowly they convince themselves that if a little is good then more is better. Even when more leads to destruction, their mind convinces them that even more will be better. Tolerance is an adaptive and fractal part of addiction. The disease, as we have seen, is in part based on the reward system in the brain. Addicts use the reward system to feel better and eventually to feel normal. This normal is not their real normal, but one that has been created to serve the addiction. They need to be reminded of what normal is, how their lives have changed. It takes at least six months for an addict's brain to start to feel normal and up to two years for the brain and body to repair themselves.

This process of iteration works against the person who is dependent. It creates evidence that builds and supports the image that addiction uses to get the next fix. Addicts either run to the disease to feel normal and "good" or they run from the destruction in their lives and the addiction offers them an easy temporary escape. The escape in itself is evidence that there is a problem, so they have to run from that—denial. This process is consistent, persistent, and progressive. The sooner the cycle is broken the better. If you are making a path in the jungle that in the end will lead you to a den of cobras, is it better to wait till the path is well worn or to stop early on and make a new path?

Just as iterations and patterns of addiction lead to destruction, so iterations and patterns that we are discussing in this book can lead to health, creativity, and remission.

The 12-step program of AA is very chaos theory-oriented as well as being highly neurobiologically founded—although the founders knew little about either. The fourth step of AA is to take a moral inventory, to look at all facets of your life and see how addiction has impacted them. The patterns are seen over and over and over again. As we help those in recovery we need to assist them in changing the equation and the iterations. We help them build a mountain of evidence that being in remission is possible and has far better outcomes on all levels than being actively addicted.

While the focus is on the present and building a positive future, we are not about ignoring the past. Dwelling on it, bringing it up over and over again only gives the person a reason to relapse. It's a fine balance between reflecting on and learning from the past and not harping on it and using it against the person in recovery.

Shame, guilt, trauma, abuse, and grief are usually part of the addictive person's life. The progression of the disease often leads to more of many of these. Shame is the idea that I am not worthy--not worthy of being in recovery. The deeper the denial the deeper the shame because part of the addict's brain knows the truth. Every lie, piece of secrecy, moment of manipulation, or destructive behavior is evidence for a deeper sense of unworthiness. Every break in a relationship leads to a deeper sense of guilt and grief. The disease will convince them that all the destruction is not their fault---but they know it is.

HOW TO USE FRACTAL IDEAS TO HELP

1. Patterns, patterns, patterns--- In recovery we are about creating habits that breed patterns of health and creativity. In the chapter called the Big 8 you will see what those look like. Support them as often as you can as they show they are doing those things. Be aware when they aren't. Those things are healthy for all of us; encourage the person in recovery to join you in those activities.
2. At some point in recovery, not the first few weeks, a person does need to take an honest look at their lives and confront what they have done or not done. Addicts are all running and recovery only happens when the running stops. This is not about guilt, it's about facing reality and truth. One of the ways to tell how committed a person is to recovery is to see how they discuss the past. Are they avoidant, defensive, or irritated? Then they are very fragile in recovery. Are they open, humbled, accepting, and direct? Then they are well on their way.

NON-LINEARITY

Non-linearity goes hand in hand with many of the other subjects we have discussed. Recovery is not a straight line from A to B to C, etc. It is part of the

163

Bifurcation process. Many decisions are made every day and each of those decisions impacts recovery and our lives. We would like recovery to be a straight line, but life happens. Stressors and triggers get in the way. Accidents, relationships, and employment all change. We do not live in a completely predictable world. The acceptance—radical acceptance—of the chaos in our lives is important.

In our lives, sometimes even when we know what we want and where we want to go, things happen. Do we have the tools necessary to deal with those changes? The Butterfly Effect is real; small changes can have significant impacts on our lives. How we are working with the Big 8 on a regular basis matters in all people's lives, not just those in recovery.

The problem with non-linearity is that we don't know where the line is going. We can plan to our mind and heart's content, but it doesn't change the reality that things happen out of our control that impact our plan. Resiliency goes a long way in determining how we respond or react to those events. For some, resiliency seems to come naturally; for others it is a struggle. It can be developed consciously and all those with chemical dependency need to work on their resiliency skills and adaptations.

What is important is to know that the process of recovery is not a straight line. There are curves and bumps along the way. Knowing this, helping those in recovery understand it, and supporting them through those times will go a long way. Having "bumps" is not an excuse to use; there are no excuses, and it is a choice they make. Learning why we make the choices we make can be very helpful. If someone relapses, what do they need to change in their lives to not have that happen again? Are they willing to seriously make and commit to those changes? Who will hold them accountable to changes they say they are making? Are there some things they can do to straighten out a few of the curving lines in their life? Addiction feeds on chaos, so we can try to lessen the amount of it in our lives or help others lessen it in theirs.

COMPLEXITY

Complexity theory is often seen with chaos theory; there is a great deal of overlap. There is a tendency to simplify addiction, to isolate causes and "cures." Complexity theory tells us that is rarely if ever the case. Chemical dependence emerges over time and varying scales, and recovery does the same thing. Our lives self-organize over time as well. We are very adaptive creatures. Addicts adapt to their using lives and in one way or another, the world around them adapts as well, often through enabling.

This is not to give an excuse for using; there are none. It is to help those helping people in recovery understand this is a very complicated system that impacts every facet of life and every cell in their biological bodies. It takes time, effort, diligence, and patience to get the hijacked brain fully back on track.

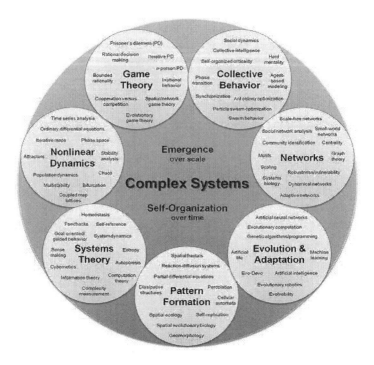

http://www.wikiwand.com/en/Complex_systems

Recovery itself is a complex system and new issues will arise for them. We want to believe that when someone stops using everything instantly gets better. That is a myth. For a time their bodies may rebel against them, their minds will be looking for ways to lure them back, strained relationships may remain strained for lack of trust, and employers, family, and friends may not be willing to do any repair work. This adds to the internal stress in their lives.

So what do we do? We understand how complex reality is, but focus on the simple behaviors--back to the Big 8. Every person on Planet Earth is part of a system that is an addict's life. We all know them. How can you help them focus on what needs to be done and not get wound up in the complexity of their lives? How can you help them stay in the moment and keep life simple? KISS–Keep It Simple Stupid—is one of AA's acronyms, and all of us could use a dose of that now and then. The person who is most helpful to an addict within a complex system is the one that brings consistency, clear boundaries, stability, and an empathetic attitude.

When someone in recovery focuses on something the question should be, "Is that concern an imminent threat to your sobriety?" If not, they should probably let it go until their brain is ready to take on more—at least six months. If so, it needs to be dealt with. An example would be a traumatic experience. We know those have an impact on addiction and relapse. If in recovery the trauma keeps surfacing and causing anxiety, depression, and/or cravings then the person should seek help immediately.

The human brain, with its 2 trillion connections, is perhaps the most complex organism on the planet. But the brain self-organizes around survival and its desire to thrive. Things go wrong with all those connections. The way to help the brain is to zero in on the Big 8 and take care of the easier parts of the brain. When our brains are "well" they will have more resiliency and capacity to cope and deal with the more complex issues. There is a tendency to focus on those first when we don't have the tools to get us through.

We help people in recovery by remembering the acronym KISS—Keep It Simple Stupid. Complexity and focusing on it distracts the person in recovery from the core parts of it.

FEEDBACK

Life is a feedback loop. We all receive feedback constantly. People, the world around us, and our bodies give us messages. Depending on the pathways our brains have created over time, we decide what to do with that feedback. Addiction has created its own feedback cycle and it isn't going away without a fight.

How does anyone change how the loop works?

1. Look at what loops you know you have. Significant loops are usually attached to triggers.

2. What persistent thoughts or behaviors are you aware of that when you look at them objectively are found to be having a more negative impact on your life and on those around you? Is the person doing this exercise willing to check out the answer to that question with others? Addicts often will tell you there is no impact of their using. When you ask those around them the story changes. We all have blind spots.

3. We continue with these types of behaviors and thoughts because we are getting something from

them. What? What does the addict get from using? If they can't admit to the pros of using, they will not truly look at the cons. We tend to avoid conflict and the negative and focus on the perceived positive, even when in reality it may not be a positive.

4. In order to shift a feedback loop, we need to change the input message of the loop, to go from "I'm stressed, a drink will help," to "I'm stressed, a drink will only make it worse, but some exercise or talking to someone about it will help." Doing this over and over again will shift the loop. Loops do not go away until a different loop has taken their place. Life is feedback; there is no getting away from it. We have choices as to what the message is and what the loop has us do.

5. Accountability is very important if anyone is serious about changing a loop. We need support as we confront entrenched ideas and behaviors. Who is in their life that can confront them with their loops that they will listen to?

6. Look at feedback they receive from others and how that either conflicts with or encourages their own feedback loops. Addicts tend to hang around addicts who support the addiction, thus agreeing with their own feedback loop that keeps the addiction going.

7. Remember the five parts of the brain that we said were significantly impacted by addiction: thinking, feeling, senses, memory, and language. What does their internal feedback look like in each of those areas? What needs to change and how can you

169

help them to do it? It has to be their choice and their work; if you do the work it won't stick.

ATTACHMENT THEORY

A lot has been written about attachment theory. Here we are not going to go into the depths of what it has to offer but will briefly go over what is important in recovery and how you can help those in recovery find more secure attachments, which are necessary for a stable, sober, and balanced life. We bring it up in the midst of chaos theory because a life lived without secure attachments does not deal well with the stressors and complexity of life. Life is hard enough to get through with secure attachments.

Many users use to overcome attachment issues. They may be fearful or paranoid of others and use to compensate and become less inhibited. They often are avoidant and isolate in their using. Relationships and the stress they may cause can become all-consuming and using releases them from that stress for a time. These are all attachment issues. Most of them start early in life.

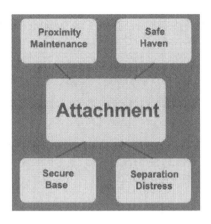

http://0.tqn.com/d/psychology/1/S/-/4/attachment2.jpg

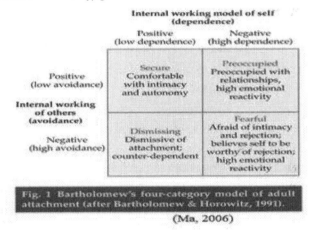

Fig. 1 Bartholomew's four-category model of adult attachment (after Bartholomew & Horowitz, 1991).

(Ma, 2006)

http://apt.rcpsych.org/content/12/6/440

Proximity Maintenance-- Humans need to have some place and someone they can rely on to be there for them. When they become distressed, where do they turn? If they turn to someone who is critical, judgmental, or unsupportive, they will use other means to cope with that

171

distress. Their support needs to be within reasonable proximity. In this day of technology that may give more breadth to distance. The idea of sponsorship in AA has to do with this notion of proximity. The sponsor is someone the person in recovery can call when they need help. One of the jobs of a sponsor is to help maintain that proximity or the possibility of it. Remember, when others do more work than the one in recovery things do not go well.

Safe Haven—We all need places where we feel safe; addicts are no different. The person in recovery needs some place and someone they can be authentic with. They need to feel comfortable saying they are stressed or having cravings. The safe haven's reply is one of empathy and understanding. AA meetings are a safe haven for many. If someone relapses we want to respond to the behavior and not to the sober person living within the addict. This does not excuse behaviors, it simply lets the person in recovery know we understand how difficult the battle is and as long as they are willing to fight and change behaviors we are there for them. To a large degree, the addict creates or destroys these four aspects of a secure attachment.

Secure Base-- People in recovery need to get back to living. They need to re-engage in relationships, work where appropriate, fun, purpose, and the world around them. They can do this when they know they have a secure base to return to because re-entry into the world can be difficult. Temptations, triggers, and stressors don't stop in recovery. In fact, for a while they may increase. At first we may need to go out with them as they get back to life. At some point they will need to be on their own-- knowing they can call or return to the secure base. Many addicts try to do too much too fast. They "feel" good so they believe they are good. They aren't. We have discussed at length that their brain is not recovered for at least six months, more likely over a year. Long term recovery views life as a marathon, not a sprint.

Separation Distress—This occurs when the person in recovery is separated from their safe haven or secure base. They are in need and can't find the help they need. This shows attachment. People who have no distress have not attached. The challenge is to find numerous attachments in recovery. Again, AA is a great place to create attachment for those in recovery. There are meetings everywhere almost all the time. Over time the person in recovery does not want to become over- attached to any one person, place, or thing. It is unhealthy for them and for the one they are attached to. It breeds co-dependency. We can encourage the person to build other attachments—relationships. This is true in spirituality as well. We become attached to our "God." That higher power that is our secure base, our safe haven, is hopefully consistently in proximity, and we feel distress when that relationship is not functioning well.

One of the ways we help is by modeling a secure attachment. What are the attachments in your life? Do you have secure attachments? What do they look like? How do they function?

SELF-CARE, CODEPENDENCY, and BOUNDARIES

Helping other people always starts with helping ourselves. If we are not well, we will be of limited help to others. This chapter further delves into the world of self-care. The Big 8, as discussed in another chapter, are things that are at the root of this no matter where you are in life. It's important to remember that you **did not cause the addiction, you cannot control the addiction long term, and you can't cure the addiction.** If you believe any of these you need to get help to work them through.

If you do believe any of these, even on a small level, you may be co-dependent on the person with chemical dependency issues. Just because they are now in recovery does not change this dynamic; in fact it may make it worse because you have become used to the user and have adapted your life to that.

Co-dependent people are those who have sacrificed their own needs, beliefs, desires, and a sense of self for another. Here are a few characteristics of a co-dependent person. As is true with most things in this book, we are not answering all questions because there is far more information on any topic than we can offer. We want to get you thinking and challenging yourself and the addict.

Characteristics of Co-dependency

Difficulty making decisions
Boundary issues, especially around intimacy
Feelings of guilt
High need for approval and recognition—to be noticed
They tend to do more and more

Easily hurt when not recognized
Find it hard to change or adjust to change
A need to control others
They do not trust themselves or others
They find it hard to identify feelings and emotions
A high fear of being alone or abandoned
They feel responsible for the behaviors of others
They want to rescue others

Questions to ask yourself—these are but a few

Do you avoid arguments and give in or become silent?
Are you worried about what others think about you?
Is what others are thinking more important than what you think or feel?
Have you lived with someone who is/was an addict, was abusive or demeaning?
Do you have problems asking for help?
Do you know where you are going in life?
Can you say "no" when asked for help?
Can you accept compliments?
Do you feel inadequate?
Do you believe you can "fix" the other person?
Can you express your feelings to others?

Co-dependency often starts in childhood, being part of a family that is not working well or is dysfunctional. The habits of co-dependency start early, sometimes as self-protection. They can take on the victim mentality. The key to stopping this way of living is to become aware of it and to show compassion for you. In brief you should be thinking about and working on the following:

-Take care of yourself--start with the Big 8.

-Set boundaries—see the boundaries section.

-Learn to support rather than to fix.

-Be helpful--- you can be helpful without being in a relationship—volunteering is very beneficial for co-dependents.

-Look at your family patterns, past and present. Often co-dependency is learned behavior and is multi-generational—you can stop the cycle.

-Find support that understands co-dependency—support groups and/or a therapist.

Joyce McLeod Heney, MSW, LCSW, CEAP, SAP offers some wonderful beliefs to challenge:

1. *I am responsible for everybody and everything.* You are not. You are responsible for yourself. You can support and encourage others, but you are not in control of them. Just as an addict has to admit they can't manage their addiction on their own, so you need to admit you can't control others. Let go of the burden you carry around that you can.

2. *I can fix others if I just care for them enough.* Sorry, you are not that powerful. Controlling leads to being pushed away and a potential sense of being abandoned when in fact it was your behavior that brought it on. You can't control a person's using for long. They may let you think you can to keep you around to enable the addiction. People change because of what happens when they use, not because you enable them and ask them to stop.

3. *I can't trust others; they might hurt me or abandon me and I may not survive.* You are worthy and deserving. All relationships run the risk of abandonment, but it is important to be true to you, to be open and honest about your thoughts and feelings. You can survive and thrive if you build a sense of self-worth.
4. *I should take care of others because my needs are not that important.* Yes, they are. This again is connected with shame and feelings of not being worthy. Your self-value comes in and through how others treat you based on what you do for them—even to the degree of feeding their addiction. We all need to take care of our needs, let them be known to others and move away from those that do not acknowledge our needs and/or are unwilling or unable to help with them. You are important.
5. *I have to help others when I see they need help.* You can't possibly help everyone. Yes, we need to help others when we are taking care of ourselves. Are we helping to "fix" them? Are we helping to seek approval? At times others need to help themselves.
6. *I am not worthy.* You are. You have immense value and purpose. You may need to find that. Shame is remarkably powerful and is used by addiction to attract enablers.
7. *It is not OK to tell someone what I think or feel.* It's imperative for a healthy life that you are able to do this in relationships. The brain is wired to be expressive. Learning to do so in ways that are not

offensive or put people on edge is a skill; it can be learned.

8. *Whatever I do I need to do perfectly.* No one is perfect. We are not about perfection; we are about progress. Learn to love your imperfections; they are part of who you are. This does not mean we ignore them or seek to be imperfect. It simply means we accept the reality that I am not perfect. I am not all things to all people all the time.

9. It's not OK to ask for help. It's more than OK, it's critical. We are not in this journey alone; there are people all around ready to help. We need to get over ourselves.

She also mentions four behaviors to work on to help overcome co-dependency. We have mentioned these before but they bear mentioning again:

1. Take care of yourself

2. Set boundaries

3. Let go of what you can't control

4. Stay away from situations that are not your responsibility

The Importance of Boundaries – this section comes from a variety of sources; we are not sure who the originator(s) is/are.

All people have boundaries. Some of them are instinctual, and some are learned. Boundaries protect us from people (including ourselves), places, and things.

Mental illness and chemical dependency tend to ignore or obliterate boundaries. In fact, they have a difficult time living when clear boundaries are set up and we stay within them. Part of the issue with boundaries is learning to protect them in spite of others trying to violate them. Like a fence that is meant to keep a wolf from the sheep--at times the wolf may jump the fence or dig under it. When that happens we would need to build a different kind of fence or find a new type of protection. We are still setting a boundary.

What is a boundary?

- It's a limit or edge that defines them as separate from others.
- A boundary is a limit. The purpose of boundaries is to keep us and others safe. They promote integrity, preserve life, and advance relationship. In the context of people we are discussing in this book, they help maintain sobriety and maintain balance in life.
- Boundaries are physical, emotional, spiritual, sexual, and relational. They can consist of the limits of what we consider safe and appropriate, our unique set of feelings and reactions, individual perceptions, values, goals, concerns, roles we choose to play, etc.
- Everyone's boundaries are specific to them. Different cultures have different boundaries. It's important to be sensitive to others' boundaries and to help them understand ours.

Why have boundaries? Below are reasons for boundaries. Under each one see if the person in recovery can list two boundaries, one they have that works and one they need to make.

Example: They give us clear direction to relationships.
 Not working: Calling "John" or taking a call from John that brings on depression.
 Need to do: Let John know not to call me and for me not to call him.

- For protection and personal security
- Boundaries help create structure and order in our lives
- They help give clear direction to relationships
- They give us the power to say yes and to say no
- To gain a clearer sense of ourselves in relation to others
- To empower us to determine how we will be treated by others

Maintaining boundaries allows us to gain trust in ourselves to take care of ourselves. It results in a healthy sense of control and overall well-being.

How are boundaries formed?

- We start learning about boundaries as infants. Some are raised with good boundaries and it becomes natural to form new boundaries. Others are raised in environments where good boundaries are not evident. It creates confusion in a child's mind and makes it more difficult to form solid, clear boundaries. Like many things, boundaries are habitual. They take time to sink in and they have to be maintained, just like a fence. As adults we make choices on what boundaries to form. Then we have to get out the tools we have and build the fence. They go up more easily when we enlist support!!! This is also associated with attachments in infancy (see the end of the chapter on Chaos Theory).

As they think about boundaries that they have that need to be fortified or new boundaries they need to create, here are some areas of life to consider.

Types of Boundaries

There are several areas where boundaries apply:

- **Material boundaries** determine whether they give or lend things, such as their money, car, clothes, books, food, or toothbrush. What material things do they need to stay away from? Money, alcohol, physical triggers of addiction and mental illness.
- **Physical boundaries** pertain to their personal space, privacy, and body. Do they give a handshake or a hug – to whom and when? How do they feel about loud music, and locked doors? What about people, places, and things they need to avoid and keep at a distance? What about spending too much time alone?
- **Mental boundaries** apply to thoughts, values, and opinions. Are they easily suggestible? Do they

know what they believe, and can they hold onto their opinions? Can they listen with an open mind to someone else's opinion without becoming rigid? If they become highly emotional, argumentative, or defensive, they may have weak emotional boundaries. What types of thinking get them in trouble? Are there ways they can build boundaries around those thoughts? Can they build healthy thoughts?

- **Emotional boundaries** distinguish separating their emotions and responsibility for them from someone else's. It's like an imaginary line or force field that separates them and others. Healthy boundaries prevent them from giving advice and blaming or accepting blame. They protect them from feeling guilty for someone else's negative feelings or problems and taking others' comments personally. High reactivity suggests weak emotional boundaries. Healthy emotional boundaries require clear internal boundaries – knowing their feelings and their responsibilities to themselves and others. No one can "make" us feel anything. We are not our emotions, but they are a very important part of who we are. Can they set up boundaries as to how they deal with intense emotion?
- **Sexual boundaries** protect their comfort level with sexual touch and activity – what, where, when, and with whom. These boundaries have to consider the boundaries of others, especially those with poor sexual boundaries. Respect for others and for ourselves is important in all boundaries. When we violate a boundary, we may be able to rationalize it

with our thinking, but our deeper mind knows we have broken a boundary and there is a price to pay for doing so.

- **Spiritual boundaries** relate to their beliefs and experiences in connection with God or a higher power. How do they see spiritual boundaries working in their life? Who holds them accountable for them?

Why It's Hard

Here are some reasons we find it hard to make and keep boundaries. Put a check mark by the ones that keep them from fulfilling their boundaries.

1. We put others' needs and feelings first.
2. We don't know ourselves.
3. We don't feel we have the right to form a boundary; others have more rights than me.
4. We believe setting boundaries jeopardizes the relationship or are told by others they will.
5. We never learned to have healthy boundaries.
6. We become convinced we can cross a boundary or allow someone else to cross just this one time-- when the fence is down it's more difficult to put back up.
7. Our mental illness and chemical dependency are not interested in boundaries, they will fight hard to not make or maintain boundaries, and they will seek out the weak links or posts in the fence and go after them.

Loose Boundaries Lead to Emotional Drain

When boundaries are loose, addicts may easily take on the emotions and needs of others. People with loose boundaries often are hypersensitive to others' comments and criticisms.

Common signs of loose boundaries include over-involvement in others' lives; perfectionism and people pleasing; trying to fix and control others with judgments and advice; staying in unhealthy relationships; taking on too much work or too many commitments; and avoiding being alone too much. When their boundaries are too loose they can feel responsible for everything and everyone, powerless, imposed upon, and resentful.

Loose boundaries may represent their own need for caretaking. In the end they disconnect from themselves, as they're not connected with their own emotions and needs.

Rigid Boundaries Lead to Loneliness

For some people, too much closeness is anxiety-provoking. Intimacy may be frightening due to fears of being suffocated and the loss of independence. Some may also avoid connection with themselves due to a harsh internal critic. Feelings of emptiness and depression may be present, along with difficulty giving and receiving care and concern.

Ultimately, rigid boundaries can lead to chronic feelings of loneliness. It can be a double-edged sword – craving connection while fearing closeness. Rigid boundaries represent a protection from vulnerability, where hurt, loss, and rejection can occur and be especially painful. We know that vulnerability is important in recovery. It is a foundational piece of working with shame and guilt, underlying issues in chemical dependency and mental illness.

Here are some signs that their boundaries need adjusting:

- Can't say no
- Feel responsible for others' emotions and/or actions
- Concerned about what others think to the point of discounting their own thoughts, opinions and intuition—start to listen to others more than to themselves
- Their energy is so drained by something that they neglect their own needs (including the need for food, rest, etc.)
- They become a people pleaser, which can build resentments
- Avoid deeper relationships
- A lack of the ability to make decisions
- Become dependent on others for their happiness
- Take care of others' needs, but not their own
- Their ideas and opinions don't matter or are not that important
- Have difficulty asking for what they want or need
- Feel anxious or afraid
- Being out of touch with what they feel
- They adapt to the environment around them, like a chameleon

- Overly sensitive to criticism—they may focus on the one negative among all the positives

How to Set Effective Boundaries

The best way to set boundaries is to just start. Try mending one they already have or start a new one. What is the plan? Whose support will they enlist to help? Think it through, write it down, tell someone else about it. Use SMART goals as a way of forming these.

1. **Know themselves.** They can't form a boundary outside the reality of who they are. Make sure they know their mental and emotional limitations. Be honest. Sometimes boundaries are very difficult to make, but they are necessary for stability and sobriety.
2. **Be flexible.** Having healthy boundaries doesn't mean rigidly saying no to everything. Nor does it mean cocooning themselves from others. We are constantly growing, learning, and evolving as human beings. Boundaries change sometimes; just make sure they are changing the shape of the fence for the right reasons.
3. **Stay out of judgment.** Practice having healthy compassion for others without the need to "fix" them. This is also true of yourself; don't be overly self-critical. At the same time be aware of when they are breaking a boundary or allowing someone else to break one. Why is that happening? What can they do next time to keep the fence up? Be kind to yourself.

4. **Accept the truth in what others say and leave the rest.** Feel what they feel and don't take responsibility for or take on the emotions of others. Give back their feelings, thoughts and expectations. Face reality. Good boundaries protect us and keep us from running. As long as we run we will not find stability, sobriety, and balance in our lives.

5. **Practice openness.** Be willing to listen to others about how their behavior impacts them. Being vulnerable means we are willing to acknowledge our weaknesses and strengths. We are able to lower our pride and accept the help of others in our need. We are wired to receive help. We are not alone in this life. When we believe that we are, we have already put up a boundary that is not real.

6. **Watch out for black and white thinking.** Most of life is gray. There is some black and white in our lives. For many those are the easy boundaries to make. Boundaries let us know where the line between yes and no lies. They have the right to set boundaries and to expect others to respect their boundaries. They have that right too. When someone else's boundaries differ from theirs, stick to theirs. Don't apologize.

7. **Pay attention to activities and people who drain them and those who energize them.** Especially in early recovery, avoid those who drain; they pull them in directions they don't want to go in, are overly critical, not supportive or understanding, or are enabling. Surround themselves with positive people who will encourage and support them.

8. **Pause.** When they feel the urge to go through a boundary or allow someone to come over a fence they have put up, stop and check in with themselves. What are they feeling? Can they allow that feeling to be present without acting on it for the moment? What do they need? Dig deep and see what comes up for them. Take five or ten deep breaths if need be, focusing on exhaling completely.

9. **Get clear on what they value and desire.** What do they really want or long for? What is truly important to them in their life? Get clear on their most important values. Use their values to guide their decisions vs. other's opinions or expectations. Use this to help them find what is missing from their life. Their value system underlies why they have the boundaries they do. Know what their core values are. See the section on values.

Ok, it's time to set some boundaries. They may have already been doing so as they work through this. Write a couple down below. Understand these are for them. No guilt around forging a boundary. Yes, they may seem selfish; remember why they are doing it: to make them stable, sober, and balanced. Are they better able to take care of themselves living within those boundaries or outside them?

Others may try to pull them out of their boundaries. Good boundaries empower them to say "no thanks." They are worthy of having boundaries. They have rights. They deserve to be respected and to have their boundaries respected.

CO-OCCURRING DISORDERS

Like many diseases in life, addiction is a difficult one to definitively point to the source. In most cases there are probably many. Over half of chemically dependent people have more than one significant issue going on in their lives. Along with the addiction they also battle depression, anxiety, mania, or some other mental illnesses. The question then becomes which came first, the mental issues or the addiction? Usually one can look back and discover the answer to that question, but not always.

When someone has ongoing mental concerns as well as addiction it is called a Co-occurring disorder or, as it used to be called, a dual diagnosis. While they certainly impact one another, they are different within the brain of the individual. Staying sober and in recovery does not automatically "fix" all depression. Those working with people in recovery need to be aware of the other parts of the person's life and how they are putting energy into working with that issue.

Addiction and mental health issues, when both active, form a vicious cycle. They feed each other. For a time, as we have seen earlier, a user feels good. The using may lift the depression or calm the anxiety. But as tolerance increases this either does not happen or works for a shorter span of time. They are rewarded by using so they use more and more. When they don't use, the mental issue in the short run seems to increase. This is because they have taken away the mechanisms the brain uses to cope with the depression or other issues. So they use in part, consciously or unconsciously, to cope with other issues in their lives. Unfortunately, the brain knows this.

The brain starts to become aware of the destruction taking place by the addiction and feels guilt and shame. Guilt and shame produce depression and anxiety, which in turn lead to more using. The cycle continues. Here is a very common view of what this cycle looks like. While everyone's cycle is a bit different, these are the key ingredients.

http://www.newbridgerecovery.com/newbridge-ending-the-cycle-of-addiction/

We will not spend much time specifically on this because virtually everything we discuss in relation to addiction applies to the other issues as well. The critical piece for the reader is threefold: a) most addicts will have a co-occurring condition and vice versa; b) they will feed each other unless both are treated; c) the vast majority of people with co-occurring conditions can lead stable, sober lives.

TRIGGERS AND STRESSORS

Two of the central things people in recovery need to be aware of are their triggers and stressors. Triggers are exactly that; a trigger surfaces and the person uses. It's like a gun, you pull the trigger and it goes off. All addicts are consciously aware of some of their triggers but they may have triggers that are unconscious as well. The addiction would prefer having triggers as a tool, and the more the better. Triggers, like the reward system, are based on habit. Seeing a liquor store, having an argument, the smell or sight of a narcotic, football on TV, or a piece of tin foil for heroin addicts are all potential triggers. More often than not in the first few months of recovery, triggers are involved in the relapse. The hope is that when a person does have a relapse they take some time to look at their triggers to see if this was true. What could they do differently to protect themselves from the onslaught of triggers pulling them into relapse? Over time triggers do calm down if the person in recovery is working on setting up new pathways for the reward system. For example, a person triggered by Monday night football can create an environment where drinking can't happen and where an alternative can that will be rewarding in a positive way. As the new habit becomes habitual along with a pleasant reward, that will be the new pathway. This goes along with the notion of a strange attractor discussed in the chaos theory chapter.

Stressors are more cumulative. They build over time and at some point we all need an escape valve to cope. Addicts choose using as that valve. There is no such thing as a stress-free life other than a person who is dead. We enter the world with stress and we have it our entire lives. Some people cope well with stress, others do not. Addiction of any kind is clearly a self-medicating method for coping with stress. In the beginning it works well. Once addicted, the biological stress the addiction puts on the person actually makes stress worse. It's another trick addiction uses. If it can make the addict feel more stressed when they are not using, they are more likely to use. We often hear addicts say, "I use so I can feel normal." Note they didn't say feel great, free, or lively; they do it to feel normal. The human brain and body are wired to be able to handle stress. They know stress is not going away and we have evolved so our bodies and minds expect stress. We all have a limit. Most of us learned how to cope with stress from early in life. Our parents/guardians had their own methods and we watched them. Stressors are like many things in life--at some point we make a choice (albeit at times an unconscious one) to let stress overwhelm us or to find healthy ways of dealing with it. There are many healthy coping skills we can learn at any time if we are willing to put forth the effort that will keep us from coping in destructive ways. All habits take time and energy, even destructive ones.

You can be helpful as the person in recovery identifies their triggers and stressors and outlines strategies to cope with them when they arise. People who claim to have neither are in denial and recovery won't last long. Those who claim they have it all under control are in denial because if they had it under control they would have already been in sustained recovery. You might ask them how the strategies they had been using are working. Again, obviously not well or they wouldn't be in the position they are in.

TRIGGERS

Have the person list as many triggers as they can think of. Depending on how well you know them, you might be able to suggest others. You can find lists of them on the Internet. Sometimes it is easier to do a checklist than to rely on our brains. Addiction is about denial; it will want to hide as many triggers as possible. The more public a trigger becomes the less power it has. Have them develop a serious plan for each trigger. For example, if a trigger is driving past a liquor store having them say, "I won't drive past any liquor stores" is not realistic. What else can they do? Remember, triggers are those things that instantly lead to using. Most people have a few triggers and a lot of stressors.

If a person is doing the Big 8, stress, triggers, and cravings will be much less than if they aren't pursuing them. The brain is the ultimate resource a person has to create and to stop the response to triggers and stressors. Both can happen in an instant when one is least prepared. Addiction enjoys doing that to a person. It knows when the addict is vulnerable and will use that to its advantage. Here are a few things a person should be practicing daily. If they do, when something happens using these tools will work because they have become habitual.

1. First and foremost people need to be aware of what their triggers and stressors are. Write them

down, and share them with at least one other person, preferably three to five. Family, sponsors, pastors, and therapists are certainly people to put on the list--as long as they are supportive and not judgmental. They need to be educated on addiction and triggers. The people that share with you need to be "rewarded." We aren't talking about candy bars, just gratitude. Their brains need to learn that it is a good thing to ask for help. When people share and allow others to help them, stress hormones are released to help the brain and body cope. "John, I really appreciate your trusting me enough to tell me this; I want to support your recovery in any way I can. Tell me what's going on? Do you know what triggered this event? Are you safe, do you need me to come over (if possible)?"

2. Find at least three people they would feel comfortable calling at midnight if something triggered them and they felt like using. This is where most people stumble. They don't want to bother people. They become overconfident and think they can handle everything. In early recovery, the reality is they can't handle a lot; they need help. The person in recovery does not want to be bothering someone constantly. The idea is to have a large enough list that they can "check in" with people a few times a week and not be seen as a nuisance. Some people only have one person in their lives. One of their goals needs to be to find more. Get the meetings, spiritual organizations, or therapy. Have them get in the habit of checking in and sharing what triggers they have faced or are

facing and what the stressors are in their lives and what they are doing about them. That might be why they are calling you. Again, like above, they need to be rewarded for checking in. "John, thanks for the call, how goes your recovery? Any bumps? Significant cravings? Thoughts you know your sober brain shouldn't be having? It's ok to share them; I know they are common and keeping them in is what relapse wants. You are on day 23, right? Fantastic."

The sooner a person in recovery learns that reaching out to others is part of life, the faster they will heal.

The reality is that those who have a very close relationship with an addict will need help themselves. Going to an Al-a-non group can be very beneficial. They are going through what you are going through. They have "been there and done that." Seek the wisdom of the ages rather than reinventing the wheel. You do not want your approach to be the trigger--and even if you make a mistake, it's not your fault. It's their choice as to how they respond to what you do or say. However, we can learn and do what we know is helpful and not enabling. This takes great insight and courage. At times, all humans need help.

When someone calls you or asks you for help, your goal is not to "fix" the issue. Let them vent; help them find a solution, permanent or temporary, to the issue at hand. Just as addicts do not recover if they are doing it for someone else, they won't learn to cope with triggers and stressors if someone else does all the work. They have to learn to go through the struggle and come out the other side sober--even if the issue is not resolved. But they also have to understand that going it alone will not work—period.

3. STRESS TOLERANCE-- One of the most common reasons for relapse, as we have mentioned, is stress. It mounts till it is too much and the person in recovery only has one way out at the early stage of recovery—using. That is the habit they have been using that got them into addiction. They were rewarded for it; the stress calmed down temporarily. When they stop using it returns so they have to use again because the physical, mental, and emotional impact of stress is not enjoyable--much easier to avoid it by being drunk or stoned or zoned out. The alternative is to find pathways that will lead to coping with stressful moments in creative ways. We know that in high stress if we can distract the brain for 5-15 minutes the brain calms down. Perhaps the most common proven strategies for doing this are found in DBT, Dialectical Behavior Therapy.

     Here is a brief introduction to DBT for those who may not know anything about it. DBT sees the brain reacting to situations with two primary centers—the rational and the emotional. In high stress or highly charged emotional moments most of us tend to go significantly to either the rational or the emotional brain, ignoring the other. Because we have both of those for a reason, this is not helpful. Wise mind, or wisdom, comes from bringing the two together. The skills of DBT are created to be treated as habits. You use these tools over and over again and your brain learns that when you use these skills it will calm down. If they are not practiced they will not work nearly as effectively. We encourage everyone to learn more about DBT either on the Internet or through some workshops—especially those in recovery. DBT has four main parts: Distress Tolerance, Emotion Regulation, Interpersonal Effectiveness, and Mindfulness.

Below is an exercise they use for high levels of stress, to give the brain a chance to calm down. The idea is very simple. A)Memorize the acronym and what each letter stands for. B) Go down the list and do something in that letter to distract yourself for 15 minutes; if you can't then go to the next letter. C) See if after 15 minutes the stress has gone down; if not repeat, but normally it will. This exercise works for cravings as well. Cravings activate the brain to focus on them and the easy way out. DBT helps distract the brain to go in a different and healthier direction.

DBT offers two acronyms: ACCEPTS and IMAGINE. We have listed what ACCEPTS stands for below. But this is not rocket science. Try this out for yourself or with the person you are helping in recovery. Think of a five to seven letter word; it doesn't matter what it is. Write it down as we did with ACCEPTS. Come up with at least two items that will distract you or that person for each letter.

Remember, we are talking about complete distraction. If, for example, watching TV is a distraction, ask yourself or them, "While you are watching, will it take 100% of your brain to watch or will you keep thinking about the stressor as you watch?" If the answer is yes, I will keep thinking about it, then it isn't a distraction. All of us know what distracts us and what doesn't.

The idea with DBT is to use whatever acronym they choose every day, multiple times, until it becomes automatic.

A--Activities—Find something to do that will distract you.

C—Contribute—What can be done for someone else; how can you take the focus off you and give to others?

C--Comparison—Compare your situation either to others who may be worse off than you or to yourself when things were better. In our stressful times we can realize it is not always like this--remember some good times.

E--Emotions--Do the opposite of what you are feeling. If you are depressed, watch a funny movie or show or watch some comedians on YouTube or do something fun. If you are fearful, do something that is challenging for you--a quick walk, crossword puzzles, write a poem or sing a song.

T-Thoughts--How can you use your rational brain to distract you? Try counting--out loud if possible, loudly. You will find there is a level of counting you can't think through. Think of your brain as a laser; focus it on something---reading, writing, listening, puzzles, origami or art.

S—Senses--Remember, it is ultimately our senses that are the origin of stress. We are not suggesting you get rid of senses, but use them for creative and healthy purposes—like distracting. What aromas distract? Put a rubber band on your wrist and snap it; you will be distracted without hurting yourself. Take a cold shower. Listen to music that will distract you. What do you like to eat that is distracting?

Sometimes it's fun to create your own acronym. Have the person think of a word with five to seven letters. Then write down something (preferably two or three things) for each letter that they could do to distract them. Make sure they include some things they can do that do not require going anywhere; addiction will use that as an excuse: "Wow, nothing on my list will work where I am, so forget it; I might as well use."

DBT offers some methods for dealing with high stress. Practice them over and over again. Look at the stressors in your life or in the life of the person in recovery. Are there stresses that can be eliminated or avoided? Stressors and triggers tend to come in three categories: people, places, and things. Focus on the ones that can be resolved easily at first. We can't eliminate stress from our lives but we can keep it within manageable levels most of the time. Addiction wants to add stress to the person's life; it is one of the major ingredients in relapse. Addiction in and of itself adds stress to the brain and body—even without external things. The goal is to get things off the table that addiction can use. This is not a call to run from life; quite the opposite, face the realities of life and work with the stressors that can be eliminated. This may include relationships, places they frequent with users, and paraphernalia they associate with using.

Recovery is about retraining how the brain thinks and how it feels or emotes. If the person in recovery is not serious about this retraining, they will probably relapse. You can go back and look at the chapter on the brain to learn more about this.

STRESS

We all have stress in our lives. The brain is wired to cope with it. How we do that is habitual, perhaps to some degree genetic. All of us need to figure out healthy ways to deal with stress and how to keep significant stress as low as we can. Addiction increases stress on the body and the brain and takes away the ability to cope with it using effective means.

When we are stressed a hormone called cortisol is increased. Cortisol flows through your veins at all times. It helps regulate blood pressure and sugar. When we have moments of stress our bodies create adrenaline and norepinephrine. These help us get through those moments of high stress and perceived threats. They are created for those moments and do not last in the body. They give you the energy and focus necessary to deal with the situation at hand. Cortisol, on the other hand, lingers in the body. Chronic stress, which is part of addiction, leads to chronic levels of cortisol, which we know leads to weight gain, osteoporosis, digestive problems, hormone imbalances, cancer, heart disease, and diabetes, and less resiliency for recovery.

Here is a summary of some ways excess cortisol affects the brain:

1. Cortisol creates a surplus of the neurotransmitter glutamate. This creates more free radicals and these attack brain cells. They literally punch holes in the cells and they will rupture and die. It also attaches to receptors and allows for build-up of calcium within the cells. Cells are literally excited to death.

2. Memory is impaired. Factual memories are weakened and emotional memories—in addiction often false memories—are strengthened.

3. The amygdala is the fight/flight/freeze center of our brains. It is where fear is located and dealt with. Stress and increased cortisol increases the number of "fear" connections and makes people more prone to be fearful and anxious of new ones. Cortisol inhibits the production of vitamin B.

4. Brain-derived neurotrophic factor (BDNF) is a protein that keeps our brain cells functioning and fosters the creation of DNF and their ability to function. People with many mental illnesses including depression have low levels of BDNF.

As we have discussed in other places, dopamine and serotonin are critical neurotransmitters. They are how your brain communicates with itself. Chronic stress reduces the levels of these in the brain. This leads to depression and increased anxiety.

Serotonin impacts mood, learning, appetite, and sleep. Women with low levels are more prone to depression and binge eating. Men are more prone to addiction, ADHD and loss of impulse control.

Dopamine has more to do with motivation, reward, balance, and pleasure. When our levels of dopamine go down we lose motivation and become unfocused, depressed, and lazy. This is one of the reasons people use; their dopamine levels are low so they use alternatives to boost energy and feelings of well-being, which in turn shuts the dopamine machine off, leading to the need for more abuse of the substance.

If someone has too little serotonin their depression is likely to also have anxiety and irritability. If it is dopamine induced they will have lack of enjoyment with life in general and lethargy.

5. Stress impacts memory and reasoning. The frontal cortex is directly impacted by high levels of chronic stress and cortisol. It leads to brain freeze and irrational thinking. Addicts know of this well, as their brain lies to them. "You can handle this." "You don't have a problem, they do." "This will be the last time." "You are doing everything you are supposed to do at a level that works." All of these are lies. As their brain is hijacked, so is their thinking. Every cognitive function is impaired.

6. Cortisol can stop the creation of new neurons in the hippocampus, which helps create and store memories. It's important for learning, regulating

our emotions, memory, and telling the healthy stress response to shut off when the stress is over.

7. We all have toxins in our system. Within your brain there is a barrier called the blood brain barrier. It lets certain things in and blocks others—like toxins. These cells check the passports of all cells trying to enter the critical parts of the brain. High stress and cortisol weaken this barrier's membrane and allow toxins to enter. It's like having someone at the customs office being extremely tired or inebriated.

8. Increased stress and cortisol are associated with Alzheimer's and dementia. There is alcoholic dementia, which can come with long term chronic addiction.

The good news is that the brain wants to find balance and, given the chance, it will if no permanent damage has been done. Even then the brain is very good at adapting to new situations. Here are a few things anyone can do to work with chronic stress. All of these at some level fall under the Big 8, but they bear repeating in this context.

1. Eat anti-oxidant rich foods like fruit, vegetables, dark chocolate, and green tea.

2. Increase levels of brain-boosting BDNF by getting daily physical exercise. The recommendation is 20-30 minutes daily—at least three times a week.

3. Start a daily meditation practice. There is a large amount of research over decades that shows a wide variety of benefits of a regular meditation practice.

4. Learn to relax in healthy ways. Try hypnosis, self-hypnosis, biofeedback, or listening to relaxing music.
5. You can also look into taking some supplements to your diet. Just make sure you do the research; don't believe everything you read in ads. There are no federal regulations around supplements. Find the science behind the products before using them.
6. Deal with the stressors you can. Don't let things build up; get help when necessary and eliminate those things you can that add stress to your life. In early recovery stress is probably the number one reason for relapse.
7. The Big 8. You will probably get tired of hearing about them, but if you are paying attention to them chronic high stress will not be an issue.

PERSPECTIVES-- Values, theory of life, 6 circles of identity

This chapter will look at our lives and the lives of the addicted from a couple of different angles. The first looks at five parts of our lives that interact and determine why we do what we do. Whether things go well or poorly, the reason behind that will fall into one of the five areas. We will not go into great detail here. If you would like to look further into this theory, check out Steve's website, voiceofsoul.info.

There are five areas of our lives that motivate us and determine how we interact with the world around us: Need, Belief, Contemplation, Action, and Feelings. This is not a linear pattern; we can jump all over the place, depending on what is taking place in the moment. As we have discussed in another chapter, many, if not most, of our actions come from underlying unmet needs. Many people will say, "I need money." The truth is a massive stack of money on a table that you can't use will do nothing for you. What you need is what the money can get for you. Most of us would not have a problem never seeing money if we could have what we wanted in life.

NEEDS—We have talked at length about unmet needs in a different chapter. Suffice it to say here everyone has needs and unmet needs can have a significant impact on our lives. How we choose to get those needs met matters.

BELIEFS—When we have a need that we want to meet we start thinking about how to meet that need. The strategies for doing so are seated in our values and belief system. Most of us are aware of our core values and beliefs; they act as positive boundaries for our actions. Addiction and mental illness deeply impact our value system as well as to cause conflict between our actions and our beliefs. Guilt comes from that conflict. If you believe it is wrong to steal, then you will feel guilty and have a bad conscience for doing so. If your belief is that stealing is fine, as long as it's from a "rich" store or person, then you won't feel guilty if you steal from them. One might say, "Then I will just change my belief system." This is not as easy as it might sound. Our belief system comes from our upbringing and the culture in which we live. When we go against either of those (even if they are potentially destructive beliefs), it causes conflict.

As most addicts fall into the arms of addiction there are some feelings of guilt. This is a positive sign; guilt is a check and balance system for the conscience. Eventually the addict will justify their using (denial). This only increases the guilt because they know they are lying to themselves. That triggers more using to cope with the guilt.

Some addicts continue to believe that addiction is a lack of will power. They believe they have none. They give their will over to addiction, which uses that belief to foster more will for addiction. In recovery the person needs to be aware of their core beliefs. What is addiction? Who or what is their higher power and what power does that have? Who can they be vulnerable with? Do they believe they can succeed? They may be at a point where addiction has rewired their belief system. It can be rewired, but that, like most things, takes time, focus, energy, connection, and vulnerability. The key to this is that it is their belief system, not someone else's. If they believe just to appease, recovery won't happen. We hear the expression, "Fake it till you make it," and to some degree this is valid. Many people want to believe something but struggle with it. We are not against "faking" it for a time, as long as there is a time limit and some people know you are faking it. The person's actions need to reflect the belief they are faking. If they choose to become a Buddhist but aren't convinced, they need to do what Buddhists do until they either truly believe it or the time set for a decision runs out. Stating you believe something and living out a different lifestyle doesn't work. Any belief should follow the values that person has. When we do not live up to our values, things happen. Below is a brief exercise for everyone, especially the person in recovery. It highlights values and the impact addiction (or other issues in life) has on them.

VALUES

All humans have values and value systems. Addiction and mental illness tend to negatively impact how we act out the values that are important to us.

Below is a list of values. Rate each value on the list. In Column A rate each value on how important it is to you. A 10 is a high value and a 0 is no value. Each value is independent of the others. In Column B rate each value that in Column A you rated as an 8, 9, or 10. Rate them on how well you (are) were living up to that value. If you are in recovery, how well were you living out these values before you stopped using? A 0 means you didn't live up to that value at all and a 10 means you lived out that value perfectly. For example, in Column A, you may have given "caring" a 9, showing it is very important to you. In column B you might have put a 4 because you haven't been very caring in your active addiction or depression. This is a pretty long list, but if you have others that are not listed, do so at the end.

Accountability
Achievement
Adaptability
Ambition
Attitude
Awareness
Balance (home/work)
Being the best
Caring
Coaching/Mentoring
Commitment

Community Involvement
Compassion
Competence
Conflict Resolution
Continuous learning
Cooperation
Courage
Creativity
Dialogue
Ease with uncertainty

Enthusiasm
Entrepreneurial
Environmental
Efficiency
Ethics
Excellence
Fairness
Family
Financial stability
Forgiveness
Friendships
Future generations
Generosity
Health
Honesty
Humility
Humor/fun
Independence
Integrity
Initiative
Intuition
Job security
Leadership
Listening
Making a difference
Open communication
Openness
Patience
Perseverance
Professional Growth
Personal fulfillment
Personal growth
Power
Recognition

Reliability
Respect
Responsibility
Risk-taking
Safety
Self-discipline
Success
Teamwork
Trust
Vision
Wealth
Well-being
Wisdom

When you are done, look at the values that have the greatest distance between how important it is to you and how well you are living that value you. In our example of caring, it was a 9 relative to importance and a 4 in how well it was lived out. In this case there is a difference of 5. We are looking for differences of 4 or more.

This can be a bit depressing because it becomes evident how addiction has impacted the value system. If you are doing this with someone, feel free to have questions if you feel what they are listing is well off the mark. "John, I see you put a 10 down for truthfulness and how important it is to you and you put an 8 down for how well you lived that value out. Can you talk to me a bit more about that? How did you arrive at that number? What they say may make sense. If you have factual information that speaks differently, it's helpful to share that. Again, the point is not to instill guilt, but to help them face reality. If anyone believes they are living up to a value, why would they change what they do? Addiction does not want people looking at values or working on improving how they live them out in their lives.

CONTEMPLATION-- So we know what the needs are and what the belief and value system are that we (they) will use to get those needs met. So what? Contemplation is where we wrestle with that question. How will I get my needs met while living within the belief and value system I want? Remember, in early recovery the belief and value system they have may not be helpful. They may need to focus on what they truly want--if they even know that. In recovery this is a very important part of what others can do to help. Listen, empathize, brainstorm, and ask questions. Just handing someone the answers does not empower their brains. There are times when they get stuck and we can offer suggestions, but in the end it is their decision. It's not fair to ask questions, get them frustrated and leave. If and when you sit down with someone to wrestle with difficult ideas or situations, make sure you have some time.

The end result of contemplation is to have a plan they can actually do. If their need is to exercise to help their body and they say they want to exercise an hour a day, you may need to ask if that is realistic. Addiction loves failure and recovery loves success, even small ones. It's better to say, "For two weeks I will exercise for 30 minutes every other day" and succeed than to go for twice that much and fail. In early recovery the time span of a goal should be relatively short. As they are successful they can increase or change the goal. For all significant unmet needs that directly impact their using, there needs to be a plan, and that plan has to reflect their beliefs and values.

ACTION—There is no recovery without action. The actions will be different for everyone but the core actions will revolve around the Big 8. Being too self-reliant and/or isolating are almost universal with those who relapse. What they need to do should be spelled out in the prior step. At times this can work in a different order. People may understand the need to attend AA meetings or some other kind of support group. They don't think about it; they just do it. But as they contemplate why they are doing it, they realize it's because they need to connect with other people; they need support, encouragement and a kick in the rear at time; and they need to be around people who are engaged in the same struggle they are. They need to be around people with similar value systems that they want to have. If you want to learn to play guitar, you don't just hang around beginners, you play with and watch experts—to learn. Addicts need to be around those with long-term sustained recovery asking what works for them and then emulate it. Reinventing the wheel is not necessary.

If the person in recovery is not doing anything for recovery, relapse will follow shortly behind. Sometimes people need to learn this lesson. We hope that after a couple of relapses they know their strategies are not working and they will heed the advice of those who have been successful.

Failure is part of life. If you never fail then you have never pushed yourself. While we will not say it's ok to relapse, it happens. What can they learn from a relapse? What will they do differently? What needs to change in their lives? Have you ever tried something multiple times and still not gotten it right? We all need to be careful how quick we are to judge. Are they trying? Are they changing what they do?

We often see that those around the addict are working harder for recovery than the addict. This leads to relapse. The addict is the one with this disease; they are in charge of action. We can help and support, but they are the doers. If they do things simply to get you off their backs, they will eventually relapse. Addiction and recovery are choices; there is no middle ground. Both take action; one is creative and one is destructive. We want to support and enhance the creative one and not enable the destructive one.

EMOTIONS-- All human brains have emotions; we are hard-wired for them. What triggers emotions and the

211

intensity of them differs with all people. Emotions come from actions done by or to the person feeling them. We can have an emotion just by thinking, but that thought started somewhere with an action and emotion from a past experience.

As the person is completing actions in their lives, emotions will follow. These may be positive or negative. Suppressing them is not helpful. Engaging them, understanding they are part of you, and moving through them is what is helpful to the brain. We have talked about DBT before and they have some great tools for working with emotions under the heading of Emotion Regulation. We need positive emotions in our lives to motivate and reward us to move forward to a better life. Negative emotions felt on a consistent basis tend to lead to relapse. All actions have an emotional response, even if it is very small. We are not asking people to be completely aware of every emotion every waking minute of every day. We can stop from time to time during the day and ask ourselves what we are feeling. Most addicts are out of touch with the wide variety and intensity of emotions. Addiction tends to either flat-line feelings or make them "bigger" than they really are. A normal range of emotions is not something we see in active users. We have talked about emotions in many other sections of this book.

Take a look at your life. See if you see these five things at work. You can start from anywhere. If you are feeling angry, ask what action led to that, how that action goes along with your beliefs and values, and what the underlying need is that is either being met or not met. They will all circle around.

Who is it that is doing all this? The easy answer is "me." But who is me? Below is one way of looking at who we are. There are a wide variety of ways of looking at us as people. This is one that has been helpful to people in recovery.

6 Circles of Identity

Here is another way of looking at how you function and what parts of you need more attention and perhaps which ones need a bit less or a different kind of attention. The idea is that we have six primary aspects of who we are that significantly impact how we act, think about ourselves, and interact with the world around us. The first three are physically located in your brain. We can point to where they occur. The last three are not. This does not mean they don't exist; they simply exist throughout your brain in a different way.

Physical—We all have physical bodies. We know that when we are not well we don't function as well and may not have a desire to function well. Some people put a lot of energy and attention on their bodies—athletes, for example. Most active addicts put little attention on their bodies. This is also true for most highly anxious or depressed people. As is true with all the circles, we can give them too little or too much attention.

Emotional—All people have emotions. Some people avoid or do not pay attention to them, but this does not mean they don't exist; they are hard-wired into your brain. Others have emotions that take over their lives. Emotion regulation is very important for a healthy, balanced, and stable life. It is an important part of long-term recovery from addiction.

Mental-- We all think. Some people overthink; we worry or can't stop our minds from thinking. Those who are highly emotional tend not to think as much; they are overwhelmed by their emotions. Our thinking brain is very important in recovery from all things because in part it was thinking errors that got the addict and those with mental illness into trouble and keeps them in trouble. But you can't simply think your way out of all situations or addiction.

Intuition—All people have intuition. Some people listen more to their "gut" than do others. There are people that rely mostly on their gut and not enough on the mental and emotional parts of their identity. Many addicts will intuitively know what they are about to do is not good or who they are about to go into a relationship with will lead to destruction, but they do it anyway. They believe their rational or emotional brains are better and more accurate than their gut, so they rationalize poor decisions. All addicts and mentally ill people have done it--all humans have done it.

Will—We all have differing degrees of will--willfulness and willingness play a large role in recovery from all things. Some think addicts have weak wills, but for the most part the opposite is true; they have very strong wills, it is simply that their will is focused on the addiction. Will is neutral, not positive or negative. The challenge is to build a strong, creative, healthy will.

Spirituality-- If you do not believe there is anything greater than yourself in the universe then you can skip this circle. For those who do, whether you call it a higher power, God, or something else, it's a phenomenally powerful circle that for the majority of addicts and mentally ill is either avoided, denied, forgotten, or under-used. The challenge is to find a spirituality that supports you, encourages you, gives you a kick when you need it, and brings you into relationship with others and with the divine (if that is part of your spirituality).

Each of these circles gets a certain amount of time and energy in our lives. Use the next section to see how much time and importance on average you gave to each while using. This is a time to be honest. Lying to yourself prolongs the issues. Denial means recovery can't even start. When you find part of the circle that needs attention, put together a realistic plan that will help it grow. Ask others around you what you might do to increase the energy, understanding, and effectiveness of any given circle in your life.

This is not about perfect balance. There is power in knowing our strengths and weaknesses. These different parts of our being ebb and flow with time and circumstance. When you are working out, clearly the physical dominates. When you meditate or pray, the spiritual gets more attention. We are looking at the life of the person in recovery overall—not in any specific instance. Which ones were undervalued and utilized while using and which received too much attention? These are all neutral. The physical body often gets the most attention for users—it's just negative attention.

View your life as a pie and assign a percentage to each piece. The total should be 100. We are looking at percentages before the using stopped.

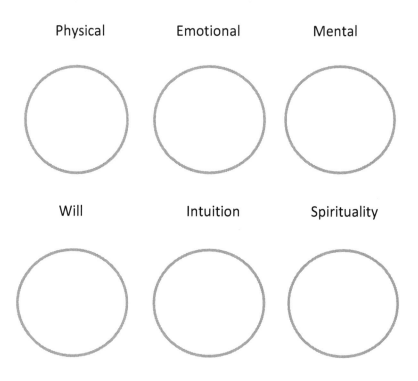

Physical   Emotional   Mental

Will   Intuition   Spirituality

The 12 Steps and the brain

We are firm believers in AA and all other "anonymous" oriented programs. They have proven over almost a hundred years to be the most effective program for long term recovery. While they were created in the early 20th century, we now understand more fully why they make sense neurobiologically. Whether someone does the step work through AA and a good sponsor with a significant number of years of sobriety, or with someone else, the work needs to be done. Because we encourage people to do the step work, we will be brief here as to why each step is important. Step work should be done over time. Expecting a person whose brain has been hijacked to think clearly is a sign that person's brain is being hijacked. Doing a step 4 before at least 4 months of sobriety is asking for the addictive reward system to engage and reward them for not being truthful.

1. We admitted we were powerless over alcohol—
    that our lives had become unmanageable.

    As long as someone believes they can control their use, they will relapse. They may be able to control the use for a day, week, month, or longer, but they will relapse and more often than not, in a big way. This step admits their powerlessness openly and honestly, not just to appease and get someone off their backs. It is followed by the necessary steps of recovery; that is how you tell if they are serious or not. They are willing to acknowledge specifically what parts of their lives have been damaged by addiction and acknowledge it is their disease; no one did this to them. It is a disease of choice, no matter what the root causes or reasons. The addictive brain does not want this. It wants a person to continue to manipulate, lie, make excuses, play the blame game, and rationalize using. That is denial. No significant work can be done until this step is taken, that is why it is first.

You can't "fix" a heart problem if the patient is unwilling to acknowledge they have one and let someone help. The reward system has been compromised and the addict is indeed truly chemically dependent and powerless to say no. The brain has been hi-jacked and addiction is running the show, increasing powerlessness.

Humans need to tell their stories; the good, the bad, and the ugly. Our stories are stored in our memories, we can't ignore them. The addict needs to face the reality of what stories were created during addiction and share them. Part of recovery is grieving the loss of addiction. Like it or not, it had become their friend. When we lose a close friend we grieve. There are things the addict will miss, hopefully more they will gain. Keeping them from sharing those stories keeps them from processing the addiction. The first step offers an opportunity to share their stories without judgment or criticism. They are deeply moving and very cathartic for those giving them. They feel relieved to get it out. Every time they share their story it will change. They will feel stronger and can make themselves and their stories more vulnerable.

2. Came to believe that a Power greater than ourselves could restore us to sanity.

Many people get stuck on this one. They use AA being a religious organization as an excuse not to go. There are groups that are more religious than others; this was not the original intent of AA. A

higher power is anything bigger than yourself—
more specifically things that can help in recovery
be it God, family, AA itself, nature, etc. The
decision as to what a person's higher power is, is
theirs and theirs alone. If you do not have a higher
power it means you are in this alone and we all
know how well that works. If someone relapses a
couple of times you can ask them how what they
are doing is working for them and isn't it time to
change strategies? Because the brain has been
hijacked, in early recovery it is not possible to out
think addiction. People need support,
encouragement and a good kick now and then.
Sanity comes through connections with others and
their higher power. As we have seen throughout
this book, connections are critical. It is often
connections that go the person into trouble---
destructive connections and relationships, and it is
creative and healthy connections that will be one
of the paths out. We know that Oxytocin, a stress
hormone is created in and through connection. We
know the prefrontal cortex and cingulate gyrus are
critical areas of the brain involved in relapse
regulation. Connection with others and with a
higher power helps strengthen each.

3.   Made a decision to turn our will and our lives over
to the care of God (higher power) as we understood
Him.

The person in recovery needs to rely on others to
help them. This is what sponsorship is all about at
its best. If they believe in God, then creating a

deep and meaningful spiritual life is critical. If they don't, then finding others they are willing to be vulnerable with is essential. This is true of those with belief as well; they can't rely solely on a God— in all spiritual traditions. "God" put us here to be with and support each other; we are not created to be islands. Trust, honesty, and vulnerability are the counter points to addiction. The brain relies on a person having these in their lives, addiction takes them away. Those in recovery need to activate their endorphins and change the reward system. Most of those with substance dependency issues are people of strong will. The problem is that they use that will for destruction because of the neuro-pathways they have created. Dopamine needs to be increased which will help strengthen creative will.

A good balanced article on the science of spirituality and addiction can be found at:

http://www.williamwhitepapers.com/pr/2006Spirit uality%26AddictionCounseling.pdf

How the spirituality of meditation can be helpful in recovery:

http://www.ncbi.nlm.nih.gov/pmc/articles/PMC31 90564/

4.   Made a searching and fearless moral inventory of ourselves.

Making an inventory means facing reality for what it is. Addicts flee reality. In order to recover, the person must face it head on----not all at once!!!! Admitting to the reality of our lives does not mean we have to deal with it all at the same time. It will be obvious which pieces of the pie have the biggest impact on recovery and relapse. This process engages most of the brain. It uses thinking and emotions to access memories and processes them. While addiction wants us to keep secrets, recovery accesses those secrets and lets someone else in on them. Yes, it can be embarrassing, perhaps even humiliating, but if they are not brought out they remain inside and are weapons addiction can and will use to bring a person back through relapse. This inventory does not delete those actions, thoughts, and emotions, but takes away a significant part of their hold on us. Memories need to be dealt with. One of the steps is to see if they are real. Memories within addiction change. At times they are completely fabricated and at other times they are adjusted. Addicts will minimize negative experiences and blow out of proportion positive ones. This step is done alone. If they have a sponsor they will give them guidance on how to structure it; what parts of their lives to look at. If they do not have a sponsor there are a lot of ways of doing a step 4 on line. Doing a step 4 too early in recovery is a mistake. Their brains are not rewired overnight. They believe it is but science shows differently. At least a few months of recovery should occur before this step is taken.

Doing a step 4 is not enough. That information must at some level become known to at least one other person, if not more. That leads us to step 5.

5.   Admitted to God (higher power), to ourselves, and to another human being the exact nature of our wrongs.

Some people will say it's enough to just tell the higher power. It's not, unless your higher power is the physical presence of others. Keeping things inside is destructive; people need to share the inventory with others. Just as they shared their stories, now they need to share the cost of addiction. How has it impacted their lives? The person hearing their inventory is to be supportive and non-judgmental. This does not mean everything is OK, you are just thankful they are getting it out and trusting you to hear. Empathy is the key to this step. We talked earlier about empathy being the antidote to shame. Telling the story and the moral inventory to an empathetic ear is amazingly powerful. Sharing is what connection is all about. In this context the person makes themselves vulnerable which secretes oxytocin which helps with stress and with feeling all right about being vulnerable. This step also potentially allows for someone to talk about memories. This can also be done at another time because we don't want the person giving them step 5 to get defensive and shut down. At some point, memories that are clearly false need to be challenged. "At work I had some issues." Reality: "You got fired for drinking." The sooner an addict faces reality, the sooner they enter the world of potential sustained recovery. This sharing affects one's thinking, emotional, and behavioral parts of the brain.

6. Were entirely ready to have God (higher power) remove all these defects of character.

In our brains the idea here is to accept the reality of change and that we can't do it on our own. This goes back to the stages of change we discussed earlier. Hopefully by the time a person has gone through step 5, they have acknowledged they have a problem, they can't do it on their own, there have been consequences, and they have done things they are not proud of. Now they need to move on. The addictive brain does not want them to move on; it wants shame and guilt to reign. How they find redemption is different for every person, but somehow they need to find it. Biblically, the idea of repentance is to turn 180 degrees. That is what this is about, fundamentally shifting one's life and what motivates the individual. In addiction there was only one true purpose, the next use. What does their new life look like? What are their purposes? What is the motivation? How are they going to shift that shift? Thinking it will just happen is naïve; that is not how the brain functions. Step work naturally, in a progressive order, enhances the brain's ability to do the repair work that is needed; assuming they are keeping on top of the Big 8. This step acknowledges connection and purpose. It continues the process of developing and deepening the new neuro-pathways in the brain that lead to sustained recovery.

7. Humbly asked Him to remove our shortcomings.

    Humility is a necessary part of recovery. Admitting they have a problem, asking for help, making themselves vulnerable not only to the addiction but to speaking the truth of its impact on their lives and on the lives of others, and acknowledging the underlying potential influence of addiction on their lives are all part of this humility.

    Substance dependent people tend to have strong wills and perceive themselves as self-reliant. Humility goes against that grain. Just as in step 1 they admitted they were powerless and shared that story. In step 2 they acknowledged they needed help and asked for it. In step 4 they made an internal inventory and in step 5 shared that. In step 6 they see they can't take the shortcomings away solely on their own. Step 7 is taking the step of action; a willingness to let go and let "God."

    To the degree people come into addiction with addictive genes and a difficult environment, this willingness (which includes being around supportive and positive people) can engage positive genes and behaviors.

Through prayer, meditation, sharing, therapy, group work, AA, or any other means, the addict's life has to change. If there is no shift in behaviors, emotions, and thoughts, relapse will follow shortly. By this step their brains are well on their way to being rewired. This is not to say that people can't fake it, they can.

8. Made a list of all persons we had harmed, and became willing to make amends to them all.

Part or this entire list may have been included in step 4. By definition, addiction damages relationships of all kinds. It is up to the addict to admit that addiction has done this. Some of the damage may include people who are dead, physically very distant, or people with whom the bridge has been destroyed. They need to be on the list nonetheless. Part of step work is getting out in the open the complete destructive path of what using did in their lives. Harm can be done mentally, emotionally, physically, spiritually, or socially. For most people, the list is not short. Like all steps, this one may change over time. The more they are true to the process of recovery, the more they will remember what they have done.

It's important to understand this is not about instilling guilt or shame, quite the opposite. Coming to terms with the realities of life is the way out of guilt and shame. These cause anxiety and stress in our brains, they distort thought and emotions, create a lower view of self which can lead to lower overall physical functioning.

Willingness is not simply voicing or thinking words, it is a deep, heartfelt sense of wanting to make things right and having the courage to do so.

9.   Made direct amends to such people wherever possible, except when to do so would injure them or others.

Making amends with all people is important. Whenever we wrong someone, our brains know it. Part of the redemptive process is coming to terms with that reality and doing something about it, facing our fears. After 4-6 months of sustained recovery, assuming they have been doing the work, a person in recovery should know with whom they need to make amends and should have the strength to do so. Doing so activates the reward system in a positive way, creates new memories, stops the lying, and increases dopamine function.

10.   Continued to take personal inventory, and when we were wrong, promptly admitted it.

Ongoing honesty is critical for ongoing recovery. Lying is one of the first signs of a movement to relapse. Recovery is about life. Once new pathways are created, they need to be maintained. Addiction is always in the brain. It goes into deeper dormancy with each step taken, each day of sobriety, and every act that is part of the Big 8. Our brains need to be nurtured. People relapse and part of true recovery is seeking help quickly when it happens. This shows they have created deep and trusting relationships, understand the nature of addiction and have reached out for help in other situations; all parts of healthy brain function.

11. Sought through prayer and meditation to improve our conscious contact with God *as we understood Him*, praying only for knowledge of His will for us and the power to carry that out.

> See the earlier section with readings on prayer and meditation. The style of meditation and prayer doesn't matter. It's the fact of putting ourselves in the presence of the higher power and our brain into a meditative state, both of which create dopamine and relieve stress. Lack of dopamine and increase of stress are significant red flags for relapse.

12. Having had a spiritual awakening as the result of these steps, we tried to carry this message to alcoholics, and to practice these principles in all our affairs.

> Those who maintain an internal sense of self-reliance are doomed to fail. Every one of the steps includes the understanding that the addict can't do this alone. If that is true, then they need to be there for others going through the process just as others were there for them. This continues to deepen the pathways, increase oxytocin and

dopamine production, lessen stress, and stabilize emotions.

Some of the information came from the website:

http://blumsrewarddeficiencysyndrome.com/articl es/v1n1/jrds-008-kenneth-blum.html

AGNOSTICS—For those who may be agnostics or atheists here are the 12 steps.

Agnostic AA 12 Steps

1. We admitted we were powerless over alcohol— that our lives had become unmanageable.
2. Came to believe and to accept that we needed strengths beyond our awareness and resources to restore us to sanity.
3. Made a decision to entrust our will and our lives to the care of the collective wisdom and resources of those who have searched before us.
4. Made a searching and fearless moral inventory of ourselves.
5. Admitted to ourselves without reservation and to another human being the exact nature of our wrongs.
6. Were ready to accept help in letting go of all our defects of character.
7. With humility and openness sought to eliminate our shortcomings.
8. Made a list of all persons we had harmed, and became willing to make amends to them all.

9. Made direct amends to such people wherever possible, except when to do so would injure them or others.
10. Continued to take personal inventory and when we were wrong, promptly admitted it.
11. Sought through meditation to improve our spiritual awareness and our understanding of the AA way of life and to discover the power to carry out that way of life.
12. Having had a spiritual awakening as a result of these steps, we tried to carry this message to alcoholics, and to practice these principles in all our affairs.

SUMMARY

We have given the reader a great deal of information. We believe in our hearts and brains that people can recover from addiction if they admit to it and are willing to do the work. No one can stay in recovery alone. We all need help in our lives, from birth till death. Just as the addict has to admit they are powerless and need help, those of us who are in a position to be of help have a choice to make as well. We hope you count the cost of helping those battling this disease. If you are helping, you will need help yourself.

There are enormous resources for the addicted and for those helping them. We hope this book provides some good practical information. Recovery is possible and life in recovery is far better than life in addiction.

Made in the USA
Columbia, SC
08 December 2019